OFF MIKE

How a Kid from
Basketball-Crazy Indiana
Became America's NHL Voice

Mike "Doc" Emrick
with Kevin Allen

TRIUMPH
BOOKS

Library of Congress Cataloging-in-Publication Data

Names: Emrick, Mike, author. | Allen, Kevin, 1956– author.
Title: Off Mike : how a kid from basketball-crazy Indiana became America's
  NHL voice / Mike "Doc" Emrick with Kevin Allen.
Description: Chicago : Triumph Books, 2020. | Summary: "Autobiography of
  hockey announcer Mike "Doc" Emrick"— Provided by publisher.
Identifiers: LCCN 2020030513 (print) | LCCN 2020030514 (ebook) | ISBN
  9781629378039 (hardcover) | ISBN 9781641254960 (epub) | ISBN
  9781641254977 (kindle edition) | ISBN 9781641254984 (pdf)
Subjects: LCSH: Emrick, Mike. | National Hockey League—History. |
  Sportscasters—United States—Biography.
Classification: LCC GV848.5.E66 A3 2020 (print) | LCC GV848.5.E66 (ebook)
  | DDC 796.092 [B]—dc23
LC record available at https://lccn.loc.gov/2020030513
LC ebook record available at https://lccn.loc.gov/2020030514

This book is available in quantity at special discounts for your group or organization. For further information, contact:
  Triumph Books LLC
  814 North Franklin Street
  Chicago, Illinois 60610
  (312) 337-0747
  www.triumphbooks.com

Printed in U.S.A.
ISBN: 978-1-62937-803-9
Design by Patricia Frey
Photos courtesy of the author unless otherwise indicated

CONTENTS

To all those who work to better the lives
of humans and all other creatures

FOREWORD

When I'm asked about my favorite moment working alongside Doc Emrick, I think about the time several years back when I heard Doc talking to someone about our relationship.

"When Edzo is 66," Doc was saying, "I hope he has someone who takes care of him like he takes care of me."

That was a "wow" moment for me.

I was a U.S. Olympian at 17, played in the NHL at 18, and was a member of the New York Rangers' 1994 Stanley Cup championship team. I was elected to the U.S. Hockey Hall of Fame in 2012.

But earning the stamp of approval from Doc Emrick ranks among my favorite moments of my hockey career. It was the best compliment I ever received. I feel humbled that Doc sees me that way because people like Doc don't come along very often.

When I think about him as a seven-time Emmy winner, all the accolades that come his way, and the human being he is, I feel honored to share a broadcast booth with him.

I joined Doc as an analyst on NBC at the start of the 2006–07 NHL season, after his longtime partner John Davidson decided to leave television to become the president of the St. Louis Blues. I tried not to think that I was sitting in Davidson's chair, but it was difficult not to think in those terms. JD is a legendary and respected hockey man. I understood the chemistry they enjoyed and I was aware of how many important games they had done together. It was an intimidating situation.

But immediately Doc made me feel so welcome and comfortable. Doc has an incredible ability to make you feel like you are the most important person in the room.

Thirteen years later we are still together, and our friendship has grown immeasurably. I've learned to love, trust, and respect Doc as much as anyone I've met in the game. He's made me a better person and a much better broadcaster.

Doc is a perfectionist. Nobody prepares like Doc. He is always gathering information, and sometimes you don't even realize that's what he is doing. He may not always use it right away, but it will come out of his mouth at precisely the right time. Whatever hockey fact I might want to know, Doc will always tell me that he will check his notes and "get it for you in 20 minutes." When I was a player, Doc asked me what it was like to play in the Silver Stick tournament in Port Huron, Michigan, when I was a youngster. I remember thinking, "How did he know that?"

What I learned quickly is that Doc has an incredible ability to tell a story without losing track of the game call. You would be surprised at how much is going on when he's telling a story. We are all on headsets and information is coming at us from the broadcasting truck a mile a minute. While I'm asking the truck to bring up the replay of Chris Osgood's great save, Doc is telling a story about how Osgood got his first pair of hockey pads from a hardware store where his dad worked.

Not sure my wife would agree, but I think I'm a good listener. That's why Doc and I work well together. We react to each other. I try to react to Doc the same way I would if I was sitting on my couch at home and not wearing a headset. If he makes some reference to Milt Schmidt from the 1954 season, I ask him, "What was the crowd like that night when you were there?"

I gently jab at him because that's what I would do if we were sitting on the couch at my house.

That's why Doc is so good. He can tell a story while calling the game, listening to the directors, and interacting with me. Nobody does that the way Doc can.

Another thing is that everyone, including me, Pierre McGuire, NBC executives, and everyone in the truck, instinctively knows when it's Doc's time. When the game is on the line, when it's the closing minutes of a tight game, when his call is all that matters, we all sense that.

When it's Doc's time, sometimes I may not talk for five or six minutes.

That's when my phone blows up. Smart-aleck friends will send me a joking text that says, "Are you working tonight?" or "Are you going to say anything?" or "I hope you aren't getting paid by the word."

But I remain silent. It's not my time. It's Doc's time.

Because I have worked with him for so long, I know when he needs to draw a breath or have a second or two and I will interject briefly on a change of possession, but otherwise I stay quiet. The last thing I want to do is kill the buzz or the feel when we are in Doc's time.

I respect that I'm working with a master craftsman, a man with a PhD in understanding which words viewers need to hear. I know people tune in to hear Doc's call of the game. As I've told him many times, no matter what team you are on, whether it's a sports team or broadcast team, you have to accept your role and execute. I accept and love my role working with Doc.

Not every broadcast goes perfect. You are going to make mistakes. It can't be helped in the broadcasting of live sports. You think maybe Ryan O'Reilly touched it, or maybe it was Patrice Bergeron. Did the puck hit the post? Sometimes you are going to get it wrong.

But when you come into a booth with Doc, there's never any agenda or ego. He is the best in the business. I can tell you that he wants to tell the story, not be the story. Every word that comes out of his mouth is about entertaining and informing our viewers.

It's fun to go to work when you love and enjoy the people you work with. And Doc and I do have some fun, like the time at Detroit's Joe Louis Arena when we won the 50-50 raffle while broadcasting the St. Louis Blues vs. Red Wings game.

I jokingly tell people that the only negative of my time with Doc Emrick is that I've turned him into a 50-50 raffle gambler. Those raffles are always for a good cause, and we take turns paying for the tickets and vow to split the proceeds. Usually we spend $40 or $50 on tickets, maybe a little more if we are feeling frisky. Doc must enjoy it because when he travels to Pittsburgh Pirates spring training games in Florida, he always buys tickets for us and sends me photos of them.

I don't remember how many tickets we bought the night we won in Detroit. But I recall there were about six minutes remaining in a 5–1 game when the winning number was announced.

I couldn't believe when I looked down and saw the winning number was the first one on our ticket.

Raising my arms in the air and pointing to the ticket, I was able to catch Doc's eye. He kept calling the game, never missing a beat, but he gave me a thumbs up to let me know he understood what had happened.

The raffle raised $15,600 as I recall, meaning our take was $7,800.

Obviously, we didn't announce our good fortune on the air, but Doc was clever enough to have some fun with it.

Here's the way I remember our call in the closing minutes of the game: adding to some of the hysteria we were feeling, Doc saw two players battling for the puck along the boards and said, "Nothing like winning a 50-50 race!"

I think I added, "The only thing better is actually winning the 50-50 raffle."

Mike Emrick is one of a kind and I mean that in the most complimentary sense. We are 20 years apart in age, but we are friends. I can talk to him about anything. He is such a caring man.

When I was fighting cancer, he would go into churches and light candles for my recovery. He'd usually light 16 candles because I wore No. 16 when I played. But if I was on my fourth treatment, he'd light four candles, or if it was the day of my 12th treatment, there would be a texted photo of 12 candles.

When you are Doc's friend, he always has your back.

Our love, trust, and respect go well beyond letting people know who is on the power play and what the teams are trying to accomplish. Something I will carry with me for the rest of my life is that I have earned the respect of arguably the greatest play-by-play man we've had in any sport and in any generation. The fact that Doc has given me his blessing means I've done something right and I am very proud of that.

Eddie Olczyk is an award-winning television commentator on NBC's coverage of the NHL and Thoroughbred horse racing, and for the Chicago Blackhawks. He played 16 seasons in the NHL and was inducted into the U.S. Hockey Hall of Fame in 2012.

INTRODUCTION

You are handed a pass. That's how it all begins. It's officially called a "media credential." It gives you free admission to the game and a seat in the press box. More importantly, it provides you the privilege of talking to athletes, coaches, and management.

With that privilege comes the responsibility of serving as a fair and honest conduit between the team and fans. You also receive the satisfaction of being able to share what you've learned from those interviews and the pure joy of having a job you love.

You get all of that with a pass. That's why I've saved each of my passes—47 years' worth. Here are some favorite moments I've witnessed with my passes:

January 21, 1990, Civic Arena in Pittsburgh, 41st NHL All-Star Game. Working the benches and intermission for booth commentators Marv Albert and John Davidson. Second intermission, I was wrapping up an interview with Wayne Gretzky.

"…words from Wayne Gretzky, who as a teenager, while playing professional hockey in Indianapolis, attended Broad Ripple High School, the same school—years later—as David Letterman," I said. "Now back to Marv and John."

"The footnote of the day," Albert responded.

"Clear," said the floor director from the studio, which was also the Campbell Conference dressing room.

The Great One knew how television interviews work. As soon as there was silence, he knew his work was done.

"You pulled that one out of your arse, didn't you?" he asked.

His teammates started laughing.

"I think Jane Pauley went there too," he added.

It was a shame Wayne didn't mention the Pauley footnote on the air, although technically Jane went to Warren Central.

February 17, 1998, Turner Sports, Olympic Games, Nagano, Japan. First ever women's gold medal game.

Canada had a limited morning skate, meaning only a couple of players took the ice. The Team USA practice had all hands on deck.

We watched coach Ben Smith call the players together at center ice and a couple of times the players laughed. At the end, the meeting broke up enthusiastically.

When Smith was asked about what was said, he said he had talked to his players about golf, not hockey.

"When I was just starting out, and my opponent and I were on the green and he was putting first, I would hope for him to miss his shot so it would take the pressure off me," Smith said. "But as I became better, I hoped he would make his shot, because I had more confidence that I could make mine, and that pressure made me better."

The Americans had just come from beating the Canadians in a major international tournament for the first time in the Olympic preliminary round, overwhelming them in a come-from-behind victory. That night, one of the inspirational stories on the U.S. team, Shelley Looney, scored what turned out to be the winning goal.

It was a thrill to call the game for Turner, to watch the American women win the first set of gold medals ever presented in Olympic women's hockey.

It was enjoyable to know that the winning goal was netted by a young woman who had overcome dyslexia. One of Looney's high school guidance counselors told her she would probably never be able to do college work, especially at those eastern schools offering hockey scholarships. Said Coach Smith, "That guidance counselor was talking to the wrong Marine." A graduate of Northeastern University, today Looney is the head coach of the Lindenwood College women's hockey team in St. Charles, Missouri. One of so many people I am proud to know.

April 26, 1998, Game 3, Western Conference quarterfinals on Fox, Detroit at Phoenix. With the best-of-seven series tied 1–1, the Red Wings trailing with about four minutes left and overwhelming Coyotes goalie Nikolai Khabibulin, Detroit head coach Scotty Bowman, rather than deciding to use his timeout, elected instead to substitute goalies.

In Phoenix, with an arena originally designed and constructed for basketball, there wasn't room for the backup goalie on the bench. That's why Kevin Hodson sat in a folding chair at the end of the rink, near the Zamboni entrance.

The problem came when referee Don Koharski skated down-ice to inform Hodson he was to enter the game—and found an empty chair. Koharski returned to the Red Wings' bench with his arms skyward, indicating to Bowman he had come back empty.

We had nothing to report on the air, but later a player who wasn't dressed for that game gave me the Hodson scoop.

"Just down the hallway, the Phoenix Suns were having a practice on the nearby basketball court," the player said. "And it was catered. They had cakes. That's where [Hodson] was."

March 22, 2006, OLN, regular season, Philadelphia Flyers at New York Rangers. This was an era at Madison Square Garden when Ringling Brothers circus performances were booked around sporting events. Plenty of quick changeovers after matinee performances.

Before this game, I asked Flyers coach Ken Hitchcock if he thought the hastily prepared ice would be an issue.

"We spoke with the elephants just a few minutes ago," Hitchcock deadpanned. "They were out there this afternoon and said it was fine. If it was good for them, we should be okay."

He was right: Flyers 6, Rangers 3.

January 28, 2017, NBC, 2017 All-Star Game in Los Angeles. I was excited to host a roundtable discussion with Wayne Gretzky, Bobby Orr, Mario Lemieux, Sidney Crosby, and Jonathan Toews. We called it "NHL Game Changers" and it was scheduled to air during the NHL playoffs.

I said afterward that I thought it would take mythological hockey gods and a handful of thunderbolts to get these five together in one room, and for me to have a seat among them. It turned out we just needed our executive producer Sam Flood, a man who gets things done.

As we walked on the set, I mentioned to Orr that if I had "never done a Stanley Cup Final before, this would be it."

No matter who you believe the NHL's greatest player is, everyone would agree that I was interviewing players who were in the conversation.

What were the chances of this group being together again for an interview? The hockey world would probably only get one kick at this can. I worked diligently at making sure my questions would elicit answers that would interest everyone. I felt pressure to get it right for this 30-minute show.

The athletes came through for me.

"I'm pinching myself right now," Toews said. "It's incredible to just be sitting here at this table."

Discussing Gretzky, Lemieux, and Orr, Crosby said, "I don't know if I could handle playing against those guys. We're a little softer."

He laughed when he said it.

Despite having his career shortchanged by multiple knee surgeries, Orr said he had no regrets.

"I didn't feel shortchanged about anything," Orr said. "I was very lucky. I got to realize the dream of winning the Stanley Cup. I'm sitting with this group right now. I wish I had played longer, but I have nothing to complain about."

Gretzky said if Gordie Howe were still alive, and had been on stage when the NHL's Top 100 players were introduced that weekend, he would have said, "What am I doing here?"

I posed the notion of a 3-on-3 game, with Orr, Gretzky, and Lemieux on one team and Crosby, Toews, and Duncan Keith on the other. Everyone would magically be 20 years old again. Orr laughed, and said, "Doc, they have no shot!"

Gretzky added to Orr, "Mario and I will wait at the blue line [for you to bring it up]."

I had fun questions that I didn't get to. I wanted to ask Orr whether it was true that when he was an 18-year-old NHL star, his Boston Bruins teammates used to make him be the designated driver, complete with a chauffeur's hat. I wanted to ask Crosby whether he kept a neat room when he lived with Mario. And selfishly, I wanted to ask Lemieux whether he might entertain making another run at buying my favorite baseball team, the Pittsburgh Pirates.

Even though I didn't have time to ask those questions, I view that roundtable discussion among my favorite hockey memories.

June 7, 2018, NBC, Game 5, Stanley Cup Final, Las Vegas. This was the night Alex Ovechkin led the Washington Capitals to the first Stanley Cup championship in the franchise's 44-year history.

Ovechkin had been a different player throughout the 2018 playoffs, playing a grittier, more complete game.

Thanks to an interview I had with then Washington coach Barry Trotz just before the game, I had the rest of the story. I knew how Ovechkin reached the conclusion that he needed to be a different player to be a winning player.

After the Pittsburgh Penguins eliminated Washington for the second consecutive postseason in 2017, Trotz believed Ovechkin needed to tweak his game to make the Capitals a better team. He decided to talk to his star and found his chance when he flew to Moscow for Ovechkin's wedding.

"I went to the wedding but not the reception," Trotz said. "The last thing the coach should do is attend a wedding reception with a bunch of his players."

But two days later, he had dinner with Ovechkin in Moscow.

"I began by explaining to him that next year is going to be tough," Trotz said. "'There's a lot of disappointment in Washington, Alex. A lot of energy lost. We're going to lose a lot of players this summer. You're going to have to dust yourself off. You didn't have a good regular season last year. The game's changing. There's a lot of people doubting you.'"

My iPhone was recording as Trotz was telling me this story. He told Ovechkin he thought the Capitals were still a good team.

"I know you're a good player, but you're going to have to re-invent yourself," Trotz told Ovechkin. "You will have to train differently. You're going to have to have a different thought process. You're going to have to spend more time preparing. Not less. You're not going to be able to take nights off. It's hard to be hungry when you're full. If you're hungry you're going to be able to do these things, retraining yourself and becoming the athlete I know you can be."

At that point, Trotz said, he began talking to Ovechkin about his legacy. Alex was 31 at the time.

"Alex, you have inspired so many kids to play," Trotz said. "They want to be Alex Ovechkin. That's your legacy. The Stanley Cup and awards, those are nice. But those don't define the kind of person you are and how you play the game. You are going to have a great legacy. You're going into the Hall of Fame on the first ballot. So enjoy playing, enjoy being the athlete you can be."

In the first two games of the next regular season, Ovechkin scored seven goals with two back-to-back hat tricks. He was the first player in the league's 102-year history to do that. Eight months later he was hoisting the Stanley Cup over his head and handing it to his coach.

I ALWAYS ENCOURAGE YOUNG MEN AND WOMEN to follow their dream into sports. Chasing my dream has been a wondrous experience for me. I've been clear about that when I have spoken to aspiring broadcasters and journalists at Northwestern, Fordham, Point Park, Manchester, and Bowling Green.

"It may sound Pollyannaish," I have said. "But there's no rule you have to hate your job. First, you get in free. Second, you get a good seat for the game. Third, you get to work with the best athletes. Fourth, you do receive something twice a month for doing it."

In the pages that follow, I have chronicled the journey I've traveled since my epiphany hockey moment at the Allen County War Memorial Coliseum in 1960. That was the moment I understood that I wanted to be a hockey play-by-play guy.

One of my objectives with this book is to introduce you to some of the many interesting people I've met, inside and outside of arenas, for nearly half a century. I hope you enjoy the read.

A COMMITMENT

If you're a hockey fan, you know the sport from the icy rink, the jersey-laden stands, and the banner-draped rafters. You know this is a sport that celebrates tradition, teamwork, and impassioned commitment.

Hockey coaches, players, and officials have a consistency of character that seems to be handed down from generation to generation.

The sport is about commitment and work ethic. You don't stay in this sport very long if you are lacking those traits.

Hockey is about parents like Troy and Trina Crosby, a legal clerk and a convenience store cashier, respectively, using their spare time to distribute commercial flyers door to door to earn money to pay for equipment and ice time for their son, Sidney, and their daughter, Taylor. The game is about hot coffee growing cold fast in chilly rinks at 6:00 AM on Saturdays or Sundays when eight-year-old players line up against other eight-year-olds in games that seem more important than they truly are.

The only heat in those barns comes from your pride boiling over when your child works for a scoring chance.

It was about a son or a daughter learning not to walk or to run, but rather to use an unnatural extension of his or her feet, known as skates, and an unnatural extension of an arm, called a hockey stick, before they could even be "a player" in a sport.

It was about your child fighting back, or not fighting back, tears after failing to make the play that could have changed the outcome. Your child knew it. You knew it. Everyone else knew it. And there wasn't anything you could say, or do, to make him or her feel better.

And in some cases, it was about your son being drafted by an NHL team and posing with famous people and having an attorney not far away to make sure his interests were represented, something that up until now you had done yourself. And you realized now his world was changing forever.

It was then 20 years after the dimly lit rinks, with the vintage Zamboni that cleaned the ice at a snail's pace and coffee that always tasted rancid, as if it had spent a week in the bottom of the urn. Suddenly you found yourself in a modern arena with 20,000 rabid fans watching your son skate on near-perfect NHL ice.

Finally, the fortunate few experience the thrill of seeing their son slip on the blue Hockey Hall of Fame blazer.

All of this happens because parents had been devoted to those mornings during those unheralded weekends many years before.

Hockey, as we know it today, began more than 130 years ago when a group of cerebral young men from McGill University in Montreal began whacking a ball around on ice. Eventually, the sides of the ball were whittled down until the sphere resembled the form that we recognize today as a puck.

More than a century later, we still use the five ounces of rubber in the oddly shaped form. That tradition remains important to us. It's also important to us that this sport remains challenging to master and that winning a championship requires a commitment that borders on obsession.

This is a sport that celebrates and rewards commitment made at a young age. It is rare that a player who starts playing hockey after age 10 has gone on to become a professional. Most of today's NHLers began playing around the age of four. The symbol of a hockey parent is a high-mileage vehicle that smells of the distinct, rank odor of used hockey gear. The smell is one not easily forgotten. It's also not forgotten that elite players, barely past the age of puberty, leave families behind for a journey that guarantees long bus rides, demanding coaches, homework and makeup work, stitches, broken hearts, and broken sticks at inopportune times. It is a journey where hard work will pay off, but only if you accept the truth that luck, both good and bad, can always change your course.

In this sport, the marquee players, usually high-scoring forwards, don't even play half of the game. Imagine any sport where the most potent threats spend 60 percent of the game on the bench. But the stamina required to play this collision sport mandates that. This makes all 20 players on the lineup card very important.

MassMutual has a commercial on our telecasts that lasts only 30 seconds. It is nothing but rapid-fire edits of intermission interviews with players. There they are. Heavily perspiring with towels around their necks. Explaining what has happened or what needs to happen.

"We stayed composed throughout the whole game...We just keep playing shift after shift...If we play that way, we're going to win a lot of hockey games...We played a solid team game...We just need to work hard...We're all fired up...We have to get the job done...We need to keep it going...We had a great start...We are keeping it going...We want to play hard...We just want to play well...We played a strong game...We need to be ready..."

The year may be different, but the game strategy is always the same.

And the closing unspoken line: "It's never 'I'. Always 'We.' Together we're greater than one."

And never is the commitment of teammates to the "we" more noticeable than when players go after the ultimate prize—the Stanley Cup.

The NHL's postseason is a quest, a mission or life goal, more than it is a tournament. Even if you successfully complete the journey, you arrive at the finish line as battered, bruised, and weary as the opponents you conquered.

It's all for a trophy you can't keep and a ring you rarely wear.

You can make a scholarly argument that the Stanley Cup is the most difficult of the major championships to win. It took the Washington Capitals 44 years as a franchise to win their first. The St. Louis Blues joined the NHL in 1967 and didn't win until 2019.

The Toronto Maple Leafs haven't won since 1967. Playoff games were being watched on black-and-white televisions in those days. It was a long time ago.

Winning the Stanley Cup is so challenging that no team was able to win two in a row between 1999 and 2016. When the Pittsburgh Penguins won the Cup in 2017, they were the first to win back-to-back titles since the 1997–98 Detroit Red Wings. Jim Rutherford, a three-time winner as a general manager with the Carolina Hurricanes and Penguins, compares the Stanley Cup repeat challenge to climbing Mount Everest for a second time.

"Imagine scaling Everest and then being asked to start another climb three months later," Rutherford said. "That's what happens in the NHL. You win in June and training camp starts in September. Because you have fresh memories of how hard it was to win the Stanley Cup, it's daunting to be thinking about making that climb again."

Stanley Cup history includes incredible tales of players persevering through hideous injuries just for the chance to raise the trophy over their heads as champions.

Everyone in the sport has heard the story of Toronto Maple Leafs defenseman Bobby Baun playing on a broken leg and scoring the overtime winner in Game 6 of the 1964 Stanley Cup Final.

Playing through injuries is an NHL Stanley Cup Final tradition. In 2002, Steve Yzerman captained the Detroit Red Wings to a Stanley Cup title on a knee so severely damaged that he had to use his stick for leverage to push himself up when he was knocked to the ice.

Former NHLer Mike Murphy, now an NHL executive in hockey operations, once played on a frayed ACL ligament in the playoffs.

Sprains. Separated shoulders. Cracked bones. Deep bruises. They are all considered minor injuries when teams are chasing the Stanley Cup.

When the New Jersey Devils won the Stanley Cup in June 2003, Devils forward John Madden told me it was July 15 before he could climb out of bed without pain.

It is not the promise of financial gain that inspires players during the Stanley Cup playoffs. Years ago, when I was a freelance broadcaster working for the Canadian Broadcasting Company (CBC), famed *Hockey Night in Canada* producer Ralph Mellanby gave me a piece of advice that I've always followed.

He told me to never mention how much players earn for winning the Stanley Cup because it really doesn't matter for them. The money is irrelevant.

Truth is, many if not most players don't know how much they earn for winning the Stanley Cup. It's not a subject that ever comes up in the dressing room. Sometimes members of the media use the phrase "trying to win a ring" to describe the quest to win the Stanley Cup.

But that doesn't capture what is really happening out there. Based on talking to players through the years, championship rings end up in a safe deposit box or tucked away, under the socks and underwear, in a bottom drawer. Players consider them too gaudy and expensive to wear, except on the most important occasions.

It is insulting to sum up the complicated desire to win the Stanley Cup as the pursuit of an expensive piece of jewelry.

Maybe pictures explain the romance of winning the Stanley Cup better than words can. A wonderful NHL playoff promotional television spot appeared in 2010 featuring players searching for the words to explain what it means to win the Stanley Cup immediately after they have completed the journey. Eyes well up with tears. Jaws quiver. Heads shake. Mouths open, but sentences won't tumble out.

Bill Guerin. Chris Osgood. Mark Messier. Brett Hull. Bill Ranford. They all struggle to explain why winning the Cup is so important, even though it is abundantly clear that it means everything to them. Blake Wesley sits in silence. Teemu Selanne is drowning in emotion.

The commercial is only 33 seconds long, but it's a powerful presentation about the lure of the Stanley Cup. It ends with the message: "There are no words."

I have been broadcasting professional hockey since 1973 and have been calling NHL games since 1980. I own a PhD in communications from Bowling Green State University. (And yes, in case you are wondering, that is why I'm known to many as "Doc.") Expressing ideas is my business. But I don't believe I have ever adequately been able to explain the pursuit of the Stanley Cup. I'm still trying to find the proper words.

It's about the tradition of the Stanley Cup chase and the personalities of the game. Suspense. Passion. Teamwork. Will to win. History. Tradition. Sportsmanship. The list can go on and on about why we love the game. Even after a hard-fought playoff series, players from both teams line up at center ice and shake hands.

This necessary interdependence produces a bond among teammates. And given the emotional nature of the sport, its propensity for collisions, and the commitment of players to the team, hockey has something else that has made it unique and controversial through its history: fighting. Spontaneous fighting is tolerated in professional hockey.

Fighting was one of the elements that hooked me on the sport. I didn't know icing and offside at first. But I understood two guys throwing rights.

In the 1950s and 1960s, boxing was still a popular sport in America, and it seemed natural to me that sports fans would be enthralled by a hockey bout. Through the 1950s, Gillette sponsored the *Gillette Cavalcade of Sports* show on NBC. We had boxing in our living room every Friday night. Jimmy Powers was the broadcaster until the show went off the air in 1960.

My enjoyment of hockey fights had not diminished by the time I became a professional broadcaster. One of my favorite memories as an announcer was a bench-clearing Sunday afternoon brawl in Port Huron between the local IHL team, the Flags, and the Fort Wayne Komets during the 1976–77 season.

As was often the case during that era, the brawl was triggered by the most innocent of circumstances.

Komets left wing Terry Ewasiuk was assessed a minor penalty and his path to the penalty box took him past the Port Huron bench. He uttered some words to the home team's players that they must have really, really liked, because a couple of Flags came off the bench and followed Ewasiuk into the box. Fighting began immediately.

The Komets streamed across the ice from their distant bench. The Flags stepped quickly from their bench next to the penalty box to meet the charge. Everybody paired up.

A few players piled into the penalty box, which was an open cubicle. No glass in back of it, allowing players to spill over the back and onto the floor.

Chaos reigned.

Wonderful chaos. Sorry, right down my alley.

Ewasiuk and teammate Dave Norris were not strangers to fighting. The two paired off with Flags player Frank Bathe, who later played for the Philadelphia Flyers, and Mike Boland behind the penalty box on the floor near a set of double doors. As the fighting escalated, they burst through the doors into the lobby, the doors swinging shut behind them.

Describing the brawl from my press box seat, I was powerless to chronicle what was happening behind closed doors.

Undoubtedly, their skates were dulling on the slick concourse floor. Lynn Hines and Lois Bush, the box office managers, looked up from their money-counting duties in the lobby kiosk to see the four hockey players fighting directly behind them.

When order was resumed, the four lobby combatants were ejected. All I recall for sure was that both penalty boxes were overflowing when play continued.

The full impact of the brawl wasn't known to me until the next day, when I ventured into the ice cream parlor located across from McMorran Arena, the Flags' home rink.

The parlor's owner told me that he was listening to my call of the game. When he heard players were fighting in front of the box office, he ran across the street to watch the end of the fight through the glass doors.

The ice cream man said that when the fighters landed in the lobby, he saw a police car speeding down Pine Grove Avenue, the main thoroughfare, with lights flashing and siren blaring. Another police car was speeding across another artery, the Seventh Street Bridge. The two cars screeched to a halt in front of the arena's main doors.

"They weren't there to break up the fight," the ice cream man said. "They were there to watch."

Although this brawl would have been considered unique because it moved beyond where anyone could see it, hockey fights were commonplace in this era. That was true in the NHL as much as it was in the minor leagues.

The Philadelphia Flyers had fought their way to back-to-back Stanley Cup championships in 1974 and 1975. In 1974–75, Dave "The Hammer" Schultz of the Flyers set the NHL record of 472 penalty minutes. Today, there are some teams that barely reach that total in a season.

Some people believed hockey's fighting style stunted its growth, and that might have been true. Unquestionably, there was a segment of society that looked down upon the fighting in hockey. Fighting is still permitted, or at least tolerated, according to the rule book.

But with 95 percent of today's players wearing visors, there is much less fighting than there was in the past.

No one ever asked me to explain why I chose to broadcast a sport that seemed to view mayhem and violence as selling points. But I'm sure a few might have wondered whether the sport's emphasis on brawling might have run contrary to my Christian values.

I never saw it that way. Right or wrong, I never viewed hockey fights in that era as being any more dangerous than playing in the game. Back then, we didn't have as much knowledge about concussions as we do today. And in 1974–75, during the brawling era of the Broad Street Bullies and Big Bad Bruins, the average NHL player was 5-foot-11, 187 pounds. In 2019–20, it was a shade under 6-foot-2, 200. With our knowledge of chronic traumatic encephalopathy (CTE) and the cumulative impact fighting has over time, my love of hockey has evolved into a modern-day concern.

During the 1970s, professional hockey executives, particularly in the minor leagues, would have been terrified of losing their fan base if fighting had been banned.

In that era, hockey fans were often caught up in the physical rivalry between specific teams. Hockey was like a morality play where patrons carefully followed the plot and rooted for their favorite characters.

Hockey games, much like black-and-white cowboy movies, had good guys and bad guys and there was no confusion about whose side anyone was on.

When I was growing up, fighters were my heroes. Before I mastered the complexities of the sport, I understood why Fort Wayne Komets tough guy Con Madigan needed to take on the opposing team's tough guy. And when an opposing player did something untoward to Madigan or one of his teammates, I could anticipate that Madigan would make him pay for that indiscretion. Every game in those days seemed like a struggle between good and evil.

A season penalty-minute total of 100 is considered significant in today's game.

Sometimes I'm broadcasting a game and I think to myself that the contest could use a fight to get one team going and the crowd into it.

But that's not the way it is on most nights anymore.

I have grown more uncomfortable watching some fights because I worry that the knowledge of Mixed Martial Arts that some players have acquired could result in someone dying on the ice.

Nobody wants to see a player go into convulsions because of a single punch. I worry now that there are dire long-term consequences to some of these fights.

Hockey fights in the 1970s were like barroom fights you would watch on television: a flurry of punches before weariness set in and linesmen intervened to stop the fight. You always had the impression that combatants were thankful to have officials there to step in if necessary.

Because today's players can be seriously injured with a single punch, I don't feel the same way about fighting that I did 40-plus years ago.

But I cannot imagine a more thrilling game—guys skating at 30 miles per hour, shooting a puck at over 100 mph, colliding at top speed, or banging into solid, stationary fences and glass.

THE SPORT IS ABOUT COMMITMENT of players and parents. But it's also about fan commitment. Once they see a game live, in New York's Madison Square Garden, or Raleigh, North Carolina, or Hershey, Pennsylvania, or Bakersfield, California, they become hooked. And once hooked, they are irresponsible with their love. They purchase gear, buy tickets, plan road trips, and ring cowbells. They shake their fists at opposing players and speak uncomplimentary untruths about the referees.

Often their waking moments are more consumed by the sport of hockey than those who are paid to play the games. They join fan clubs, call talk shows, sing praises, and conjure up startling trade proposals.

On a 95-degree day in July, they will begin counting the days until hockey training camps begin. You wonder if they have lives. They do. And they wouldn't trade it for anything.

Neither would I. That's why I have been a hockey broadcaster for 47 years.

2

GOLD MEDALS, THE CORN KING, AND FIVE-MINUTE NEWS

"Shoot on this guy from anywhere. I repeat: Shoot. On. This. Guy. From. Anywhere."

Those were the words of my partner Eddie Olczyk during the 2010 Olympic men's hockey gold medal game in Vancouver, between the United States and Canada. It was watched by the largest audience I'd ever had as NBC's play-by-play man.

Eddie was referring to Canadian goalie Roberto Luongo, figuring the Americans were "going to school" on Luongo who was "obviously not comfortable" in the goal crease.

That game is one of more than 3,750 hockey games I have been privileged to call. For me, that game had all of the elements that make the sport magnificent: the outcome in doubt (Canada led 2–1 in the final minute), the goalie pulled (gallant USA netminder Ryan Miller on the bench for the extra attacker), and no one leaving the arena, as their hearts race because of the thrilling plays around the net.

With 25 seconds left in regulation, Zach Parise tied the game for Team USA. The gold medal game went to overtime.

More magnificence. The anticipation and speculation. Who would score the winning goal? How long would it take? Answer: Canada's Sidney Crosby, on Miller at 7:40 into overtime.

My last words were: "The gold medal to Canada." And then about 100 seconds of exceptional television; the noise of the crowd, brilliant pictures of elation and disappointment, and the exhaustion of both teams.

Pierre McGuire, NBC's "Inside the Glass" commentator, interviewed both Crosby and Miller. The teams were still on the ice because medals were going to be presented.

Both men spoke with class and respect for their teammates and their opponents. Had the result gone the other way, I am confident the same two guys would have provided the same tone.

I cannot remember a time when I was prouder to be associated with the sport, calling a game from one of North America's largest cities before a huge U.S. television audience.

When I think back to my life in an Indiana town of 627 people, I am shocked, lucky, blessed, grateful, and mystified that I have had a seat—for free!—for so many wonderful and unusual moments.

I was wearing a headset microphone when Crosby scored a shootout winner during a snowfall in the NHL's first Winter Classic in Buffalo. I have gotten to be outdoors in 18 other NHL games. I also got to be there when Team USA won the first Olympic women's gold medal for hockey in Nagano, Japan, in 1998, and in water polo, in London, in 2012. I was also the privileged wearer of a microphone when Brett Favre threw the first of more than 8,500 passes for the Packers, when Wayne Gretzky took three curtain calls after his final game in 1999, for 22 Stanley Cup Finals, and 14 All-Star Games.

Now, in golf terms, I'm using a pitching wedge on the back nine. But I would not trade my time on the course, especially those early entries on my scorecard, for anything.

Including life in that town of 627.

GROWING UP IN LaFONTAINE (PRONOUNCED LA-FOUNTAIN), Indiana, in the 1950s, I didn't see much playoff hockey. Everyone who has watched the movie *Hoosiers* understands that Indiana was a basketball state, especially in that era.

During the 1950s, the good people in Indiana were far more interested in the high school state basketball tournament than they were in hockey. Not much NHL news flowed into LaFontaine, a small town that has had its own post office since 1858, but has never seen its population swell above 1,000, according to the U.S. Census Bureau.

Located on State Road 15, LaFontaine was such a small town that it would have been possible to see one city limit sign from the other if not for a bend in the road on the flat Hoosier terrain and the towering presence of two grain elevators.

The most famous citizen of LaFontaine was Chester E. Troyer, the man some folks dubbed "The Corn King." He made a name for himself by showing grand champion ears of corn at the International Grain and Hay Show in 1920, 1927, 1932, and 1939. He was one of the early producers of hybrid seed corn.

The high school basketball team was always the talk of the town. Reba Troyer, one of the more vibrant middle-aged members of the Troyer family, had no kin on the squad, but she attended most games. She bought a season ticket that allowed her to sit in the front row of the bandbox compact floor, with her toes touching the out-of-bounds line. That gave her the perfect placement to mercilessly harass the referees after every decision that went against LaFontaine. She often wore a dress coat, which was usually removed so she could shake it at the official to let him know she was unhappy with his judgments on the court—and it better be different next time.

LaFontaine was not a town that was paying much attention to the small number of NHL games CBS was televising on the weekend. But I was watching those games in snowy black and white, and listening to Bob Chase's radio broadcasts of the Fort Wayne Komets.

IN INDIANA, WHERE BASKETBALL HAS always been king, I spent my early childhood as a baseball guy.

The population of LaFontaine was under 700 when I was in grade school. In the 1950s, I might have been the only Pirates fan in Central Indiana. Thanks to KDKA's powerful radio signal, I was able to listen to Bob Prince call their games on a nightly basis in the summer months.

"Kiss it good-bye," Prince would offer when Roberto Clemente would club a fastball over the left-field fence.

I listened regularly to Prince and color man Jim Woods make baseball seem like a sport of wonder and romance. In the 1950s and 1960s, a boy's first love was often baseball.

The Emrick front yard was our ballpark. My brother, Dan, transformed a piece of quarter-inch plywood into a replica scoreboard as a shop class project at LaFontaine High School. After taking careful measurements, I hammered nails into the right spots to allow for the hanging of an inning-by-inning run count. To us, it was just like the scoreboard at Wrigley Field.

Baseball announcing soon became my ambition. Dan and I would play nine-inning simulated games on our front lawn, complete with major league lineups, filled out and mimeographed, and radio-quality broadcasting. Or so we thought.

Dan loved the Dodgers and the Pirates were my team. Most times we avoided those two teams, and we never allowed them to play against each other. When Duke Snider was up for Dan's Dodgers, I would have to move into right field, because the left-handed-hitting Snider would hit the ball there most often. When Clemente was batting for my Pirates, Dan would be stationed in left field.

The ball would be tossed in the air and driven into the outfield, and as one of us would race to flag it down, the other would describe the action in a style that we had copied and honed while listening to the Chicago Cubs' Jack Quinlan or the Cincinnati Reds' Waite Hoyt or the Chicago White Sox's Bob Elson.

I enjoyed hearing Elson describing a home run with his signature call: "And it's a White Owl wallop, and a box of cigars for Larry Doby."

When we played those baseball games in front of our house, Dan's Dodgers and my Pirates never lost and those evil New York Yankees (aka the world champions) never won.

These ballgames were two-man operations, although the family German shepherd, Jill, was incorporated into both the game and the rules.

Jill would crouch 10 feet from home plate, and then bolt at the crack of the bat toward the outfield in pursuit of the baseball. If she snagged the ball before the outfielder could chase it down, then it was considered a ground-rule double. More than once a sure Pee Wee Reese triple was turned into a canine double because the outfielder wasn't fast enough, or well-conditioned enough, to outperform Jill.

Each of our game balls had canine incisor marks.

Looking back, my brother and I lived an idyllic life. My father, Charles, was a high school principal and my mother, Florence, was a home economics and gym teacher. We also owned a music shop in nearby Wabash. Whenever the store sold a piano or organ, my brother and I were usually involved in delivering it. It was worth the trouble, because the sale of a piano or organ also meant the family would have steak for dinner.

Even though LaFontaine was a small town, it seemed as if we regularly had major news events happening. When I was in fifth grade, the controversial firing of popular high school basketball coach Charlie Steidle caused a town-wide insurrection.

Indianapolis TV station WFBM (Channel 6) sent a photographer to LaFontaine to report the story.

LaFontaine High School students were shown on Gilbert Forbes' nightly newscast walking out of the school in the middle of the day to protest "Charlie being fired."

The protesters marched three blocks to LaFontaine's "downtown," which was a strip of businesses one block long.

Trustee Bob McKinley had fired Steidle, and the fact that the two men happened to own the town's only two restaurants made the story juicier.

For a youngster interested in a career in the media, the furor over a man's firing was fascinating. The story grew so big that an assembly was scheduled in the high school gymnasium when a resolution was reached.

Everyone was invited, even the fifth-graders. The high school band and chorus were both brought in to perform. Then McKinley strode out, stood next to the piano, and announced Steidle had been reinstated.

He finished his speech with an Abraham Lincoln quote: "With malice toward none, with charity for all."

With great emotion, he slapped his hand down on the piano and strode off.

The attendees erupted in jubilation. A standing ovation. Might have been the most dramatic moment in the town's history.

The only news event that might have rivaled the Steidle revolt occurred three years later. When I awoke three days after Christmas in 1961, my mother had a question for me.

"Do you have anything of value at the LaFontaine school?" she asked.

"Just my clarinet," I said. "Why?"

"The school burned to the ground last night," she said.

The fire had started in our beloved, hallowed gymnasium and spread rapidly. The building had been erected in the 19th century. Fire departments from the nearby towns of Wabash and Marion assisted the LaFontaine volunteers fighting the blaze in subfreezing temperatures.

Only a recently constructed four-room wing—with the band room and my clarinet—escaped the flames.

Arson was suspected. It's been 58 years since the fire, but if you travel to LaFontaine today somebody there will give you the name of his or her prime suspect. The school was important to the town. People haven't forgotten the night it was lost.

And, in case you are wondering, our entire family was out of the LaFontaine area that night. We went to the Coliseum to see the Komets play the Omaha Knights. I have the ticket stubs to prove it.

MY HEART REMAINED ON THE diamond, not the ice, until December 10, 1960, when my broadcasting ambitions were reborn.

That was the night my parents took us to the big city of Fort Wayne to see my first live hockey game.

It was an International Hockey League game between the Fort Wayne Komets and Muskegon (Michigan) Zephyrs.

Every Indiana garage and barn has a rim attached, and each small town has stories about a player or two from yesteryear who could shoot the lights out like Jimmy Chitwood in *Hoosiers*. We didn't have a Chitwood, but we were hoping he would show up soon.

Around town, most boys were working on their jumpers while my brother and I were honing our hitting skills. Being on the LaFontaine High School basketball team was a dream for most kids in the town. The town's energy flowed from the LaFontaine Cossacks during the winter months. No one was bothered by the irony that we had a Russian nickname during the Cold War. It had probably been adopted during the time of the Czar anyway.

In the 1950s and 1960s, hockey was foreign to most Hoosiers. All I knew about the sport came from watching a few Saturday afternoon games on CBS and listening to legendary broadcaster Bob Chase call the sometimes fight-filled Komets games on WOWO, the powerful 50,000-watt radio station that reached 36 states and six Canadian provinces at night.

It was a 45-mile drive from LaFontaine to the Allen County War Memorial Coliseum. We had been there before to watch Holiday on Ice. But I was confident that watching an IHL game would be far more satisfying. An excitement built within me as our 1959 red Plymouth station wagon navigated Route 124.

The impact of that first trip to see the Komets more than a half century ago is evidenced by how much detail I recall about it.

Snow had fallen days before and I remember the Indiana countryside looked like the front of a Christmas card. Undisturbed, wind-driven snow covered the farmland, interrupted occasionally by a few homes with Christmas lights sagging from gutters and arches. Snow shovels leaned against porch railings. Children's sleds parked in the front yard ready for the next day's adventures. It was around 5:00 PM, but we were in the Central time zone, approaching the shortest day of the year, meaning it was already dark. But the whiteness of snow seemed to illuminate the picturesque surroundings.

It was a family night out, and that meant we stopped at Colonel Sanders Hobby Ranch House for a family style chicken-and-ham dinner.

The Colonel's meals were always scrumptious, but dining there was the reason we didn't arrive at the Coliseum until after warm-ups had been completed. We were first-timers and simply didn't know any better.

As we settled into our seats, located on the blue line in the lower bowl, the Zamboni—sponsored by Seyfert's, the local potato chip manufacturer—was scraping the ice and dumping snow in the huge open bin above the wheels.

What struck me immediately was that the Coliseum, constructed in 1952, looked far more wondrous as a hockey arena than it had as the location for Holiday on Ice.

The Coliseum was only eight years old but already had history and importance in Indiana sports lore. The NBA's Detroit Pistons started as the Fort Wayne Pistons and played at North Side High School's gym at their inception in 1948. They moved to the Coliseum when it was built in 1952 and played there until moving to Detroit in 1957.

To a 14-year-old, the Coliseum had a magical presence. As we walked up a series of ramps to reach our seats, you could hear employees hawking the Komets' 16-page program.

"Komet Hockey Lucky Number Souvenir Program!" the workers yelled. "Only 25 cents!"

You could feel the buzz about the game the moment you walked through the turnstile.

Settling into our seats with the 8:00 PM opening faceoff fast approaching, I had far more questions than I had answers.

At that point in my life, I didn't know the difference between offside and icing. I wondered why the Zamboni didn't chew up line markings. I wondered if the chicken-wire screens above the boards were in place just to protect the fans from flying pucks, or whether it was also to keep players who were faint of heart from leaving when the game turned wild.

I had listened to Bob Chase call enough games on WOWO to know that IHL games could sometimes include parades to the penalty box.

I spotted Norm Carroll seated at the powerful Coliseum organ. From listening to games on the radio, I knew that when an opposing player drew a penalty, Carroll would sometimes take "musical jabs."

Since Christmas was coming, I was hoping Carroll would play "Santa Claus Is Coming to Town"—"You better watch out, you better not cry, you better not pout"—when a Muskegon villain entered the penalty box, saving the very last note to play when the player's behind reached the penalty box seat.

Every aspect of my first hockey night exceeded my heightened expectations. I spotted the 6-foot-4 Chase standing in the press box, speaking into a headset microphone.

When the Zephyrs came out, splendidly attired in their blue uniforms, it struck me that the color was the brightest blue I had ever laid eyes upon.

The team fight song that season was "Buckle Down Winsocki" and Carroll's rendition was stirring as the Komets rushed onto the ice in their black pants and white jerseys, with their memorable orange cartoon spaceman looking splendid on the front.

Fans stood and cheered when Fort Wayne goalie Reno Zanier entered the crease and began scraping up the ice with his skates, like a warrior preparing his fortification for the pending battle. In 1959, Jacques Plante had changed the NHL forever by donning a mask in a game for the Montreal Canadiens. But IHL goalies apparently hadn't received the memo because Zanier was fearlessly barefaced as the puck was dropped.

Zanier and other players were three phone calls away from ever landing in the six-team NHL, but you would have never known that by how hard they competed that night. The speed was spellbinding. The intensity was astonishing. The collisions had the explosiveness of fireworks. More than once, players went flying into the wire fences.

It was as if someone had written a script that would allow a 14-year-old to have a perfect experience at a hockey game.

One player I knew well from listening to Komets games on the radio was rugged Cornelius "Con" Madigan. He was a perennial penalty-minutes leader and the toughest fighter on the Fort Wayne squad. In 1959–60, he posted seven goals and 272 penalty minutes.

But on this night, Madigan would be an offensive hero. Trailing by a goal with under a minute to go, the Komets pulled their goalie and noted pugilist Madigan produced the tying goal.

What I learned that night was that Madigan was always so excited about scoring that he would skate around the rink backward after each of his goals.

At that point, it didn't seem possible that the game could get more entertaining. But in the final seconds of the 10-minute overtime period, Madigan squared off to fight Morris "Moose" Lallo, who was Muskegon's toughest competitor.

The only experience my brother and I had with "fighting" was what we saw on the staged *All-Star Wrestling* show, when Dick the Bruiser and Crusher Lisowski would take on "peroxide blond" brothers Roy and Ray Shire in a sport that was clearly more entertainment than competition.

Lallo vs. Madigan was far different. I remember thinking, "Those are real punches those players are throwing!"

As we trudged across snow-crusted ice in the Coliseum parking lot after the game, I knew I had just witnessed a life-altering event. It was the sports equivalent of a religious conversion. Went to that game aspiring to be a baseball broadcaster. Left the game believing fervently that I had a different calling.

I had been enchanted by Waite Hoyt's ability to tell Babe Ruth stories during rain delays. Whenever possible, I wanted to hear Chicago Cubs radio man Jack Quinlan, whose partner was Hall of Famer Lou Boudreau. I often thought about how wonderful my life would be if I could end up behind a baseball microphone.

But my ambitions changed after seeing those Fort Wayne players in their spaceman jerseys play a hockey game. As it turned out, the $2.50 my parents paid for my seat at the Komets game was the best investment they could have made in my future.

RECEIVING MY DRIVER'S LICENSE AT age 16, and trusting parents, also helped put me on the path toward becoming a hockey broadcaster.

They allowed me to travel to Fort Wayne on my own to watch Komets games. Sometimes some of my buddies would miss our high school's road basketball games, which was considered a venial sin in Indiana, to be part of the Komets' Saturday-night sellouts.

Today, I tell young broadcasters to take advantage of every opportunity to get behind a microphone. Get yourself in front of people, make mistakes, be nervous, and learn from every experience. I tell them that because that was the path I followed. You'll still make some mistakes, but you won't make the ones you made before.

The great educator and musician Shinichi Suzuki said: "Skill is knowledge, plus doing something 10,000 times."

I embraced the law of averages when I was young. I made as many mistakes as possible, hoping I would make fewer as I grew older and wiser.

When my high school needed an announcer for home basketball games, I enthusiastically volunteered. I did that for three full seasons. One of the attendees at those games was Rosemary Eppley, a newscaster on the local Wabash radio station. She must have liked the way I sounded, because when the station needed someone on Saturday and Sunday to deliver the news to their listeners, she thought of me.

Now, as a high school senior, I was gathering, writing, editing, and delivering local news for WARU. My pay was $5 for each day. All that mattered to me was that at 17, I was a professional broadcaster.

Wabash was then, and remains, a town of 10,000 citizens. In the 1960s, it was mostly inhabited by law-abiding souls, which meant there weren't many days filled with major news events. Our studio was located on the edge of town, and our transmitter was stationed 15 miles west, in the city of Peru. I was set up in the studio, and at 12:10 PM on Saturday and Sunday, the announcer in Peru would throw a switch and I would spend five minutes delivering the news from the Wabash studio.

My news-gathering process in peaceful Wabash consisted of first visiting the fire department to collect information about their runs and resuscitations. Then, I stopped at the police station, sheriff's office, and jail to see what was happening there. If I needed to pad the stories to fill the five minutes, I would give names, age, and car accident descriptions, even if it was just a fender-bender with damage under $100.

Mortuaries would also pay us $1 to report an obituary. On quiet weekends, my news roundup would often conclude with "Friends may call between 10:00 AM and noon..."

Soon, while still in high school, I was promoted to the main studio in Peru to fill the Sunday morning shift. Not many people wanted that job because it meant driving to work at 4:30 in the morning and signing on by 6:00 AM. I started by bringing up the pre-recorded "Hour of the Crucified" and continued through the live broadcast of the First Baptist Church that began at 11:00 AM. During my Sunday morning shifts, I was the only person in the studio.

This was important programming to WARU because it was a "daytime" station, meaning it could broadcast only until the sun set locally. In December, the station signed off at 5:15 PM, and in the summer months we stayed on until 8:15.

After high school graduation, I also worked weekdays as host of the "Sundown Serenade" show. It was promoted as "music for when the day is done."

"Wacky" Dave Walrod was chief engineer and host of the "Big Sound Survey" rock show. He signed off to me at 6:00 PM. Talk about a tough act to follow—it was like driving into a wall every day. Our listeners went from listening to the sizzling-hot Beatles, Elvis Presley, and the Dave Clark Five to my offerings of the Living Strings, Mantovani's orchestra, and Tony Bennett.

I would not have wanted to see the Nielsen numbers on my program.

It was said that my job was to play anything "without a beat." Another WARU host, Mike Reinhart, used to say that my job "was to put people to sleep."

One odd duty that the "Sundown Serenade" host also had to fulfill every day was to gather and then burn the daily trash.

Back then, radio and television stations and newspapers had teletype machines loudly spitting out the news continuously. They generated reams of printed material daily, and it was important to remove and dispose of it promptly.

Once the trash was gathered, I hauled it down the stairs and outside to a small, fenced-in area near an open field. You lit a match and your job was done. Simple task. Or so I thought.

One afternoon, I arrived at the station and was summoned to the office of general manager Dick Schultz. I knew this was coming. A fellow staffer had informed me that "Chief wants to see you when you get in because you set the field on fire last night."

Just like I always did, I torched the trash, assumed all was well, then drove the 15 miles home for an uneventful night.

Meanwhile, back in Peru, the fire department had to extinguish the field fire that had started when my trash embers blew into it. This was the field surrounding our station's transmitter tower.

The boss was understanding.

"Be careful with the trash and matches, OK?" he said.

Yes, Smokey, I sure will. I didn't say that but that's what I was thinking. I was young.

IN THE FALL OF 1965, I headed to Indianapolis to take advantage of a four-year half-tuition scholarship to prestigious Butler University. I enrolled with the intent of being a radio major.

That didn't work out very well.

Although I made the Dean's list, with two As, two Bs, and two Cs in my first semester, I decided to toss away a valuable scholarship and transfer to Manchester College, a liberal arts school located in North Manchester, about 30 minutes from LaFontaine.

It was not a step I took lightly. My decision to switch schools was based on many factors. Upon arrival at Butler, I discovered, despite my previous experience, that it was unlikely I could find work at WAJC, the booming FM voice of the school.

I knew Butler didn't have a television station, but I was looking forward to at least taking a television class there. It is a prestigious school, and I'm sure it has a modern media approach today. But in 1964 the TV course included the use of "cameras" that were actually rectangular plywood boxes mounted on 2x4 tripods. Four furniture rollers were inserted to allow for the quick movement of the cameras during a show. Each wooden camera had a piece of stiff garden hose on the back to serve as a handle.

Even though I was young and didn't know all that much about the business, I knew Butler at that point didn't meet my expectations for a school.

By transferring, I figured I could work at a commercial station on the weekends and perhaps earn a shot at broadcasting sports at the college station.

My decision to change schools couldn't have worked out better. I was hired by WBAT in Marion, which was a bigger city than Peru. I had been making $1.25 an hour at WARU, and I received a raise to $1.35 per hour in Marion.

The station general manager was a colorful, bombastic man named Bill Fowler who was called the "voice of the Marion Giants." That was the local high school team.

Fowler told me he needed someone to be the summer fill-in and work Sunday mornings all year. I told him I enjoyed the Sunday morning shift.

He told me his first radio job, decades before, was providing an introduction for a live broadcast for the First Friends Church Sunday service in Marion. One Sunday morning, in the 1940s, Fowler, with his headset on, opened his microphone and read: "It's 11:00, and we now join the live service of the First Friends Church, 7th and Adams, in Marion."

He pushed the switch and heard nothing. He raised the volume. Still no service. He jiggled the switch once, twice more, but all he had was dead air.

Forgetting his microphone was live, Fowler said: "Well, what the hell has gone wrong now?"

Eventually, he figured out what was wrong and fixed it. The church service came to life on WBAT. At that point, his only concern was whether anyone had heard him cuss on air before the service started.

He quickly got his answer.

The phone rang, and a female listener made it clear that she had heard him vent his frustration.

"I don't think what your announcer just said on the air was very appropriate or nice," she said. "Especially right before a church service!"

Thinking quickly on his feet, the young Fowler said: "Ma'am, you are 100 percent right. In fact, we just fired him."

As a sophomore at Manchester, I was named sports director of the campus station. That title came with an opportunity to do some play-by-play of Manchester football and basketball games. The campus station was a common-carrier facility, wired into dormitories and buildings.

While we had a limited audience, it was another opportunity to make mistakes and learn from them.

In my junior year, I become station manager. It was an opportune time to have that title because we became an over-the-air FM station. We had to send in five recommendations for call letters to the Federal Communications Commission (FCC).

Our advisor, Ron Aungst, came up with four suggestions, all of them including the letters "MC" for Manchester College.

As a fifth choice, he used the standard "W" followed by initials of the last name of his last three station managers: Brent Barkman, Dave Kistler, and Mike Emrick.

WBKE.

It was a throwaway entry, created merely to fulfill application requirements.

You know where we are going with this: the government chose the throwaway call letters. To this day, the FM station at Manchester is WBKE.

Because Manchester was only an hour from Fort Wayne, I was able to continue attending Komets games. I still sat alone and called games into a portable reel-to-reel tape recorder. I would listen to the tape on the ride home. Then, I would put away the tape for a month. By the end of the month, I would have forgotten what happened in the game. Only then could I listen to the tape and determine whether I was doing an adequate job of describing the play.

In my final year of earning a bachelor's degree in speech, I proposed a half-hour edited radio program on sports broadcasting. My idea was accepted.

To learn about the business, I contacted Fort Wayne sportscaster Len Davis, who had done football and basketball play-by-play for decades on WGL radio, plus Hilliard Gates, station manager and sports director of WKJG-TV. You can still see and hear him do play-by-play if you watch *Hoosiers*; he plays the broadcaster in the state games.

My third choice for an interview subject was my idol, Chase.

As I recall, Davis provided encouragement. He basically said, "Keep doing games, even to yourself, and don't quit."

That's similar advice to what I tell young broadcasters today.

A lucky last question to Gates gave me a memorable story for my program.

"What's the most unusual event you ever broadcast?" I asked as I was wrapping up the interview.

He replied that he broadcast the lowest-scoring game in NBA history.

Gates was the Pistons broadcaster on November 22, 1950, when they defeated the Minneapolis Lakers 19–18 in the Minneapolis Auditorium.

The Lakers boasted the NBA's best player in George Mikan, a 6-foot-10 center who led the NBA with a 28.4 points-per-game average that season. Mikan was also a strong rebounder and the Lakers liked to keep him near the basket to take advantage of that fact.

"Our coach, Murray Mendenhall, was certain the Lakers were playing an illegal zone defense," Gates told me. "So he told the team before the game, 'The first time we bring up the ball, Larry [Foust], you go to the key and we will get you the ball. If Mikan comes out to guard you, that's man-to-man and we will play basketball. If Mikan doesn't come, that's a zone.'"

The plan was for the Pistons to hold the ball if Mikan didn't come away from the basket. That's what happened.

In that era, the NBA had no 24-second shot clock. The Pistons were able to hold the ball for minutes at a time. The score was 13–11 at halftime.

After the Pistons pulled out the one-point win, security personnel hustled Gates away from the floor.

"They locked us all in the Pistons dressing room because the crowd was so irate," Gates told me.

As a result of that game, NBA team officials reportedly had a gentleman's agreement not to play that way ever again. In 1954, the NBA officially adopted a 24-second shot clock, which forced a team to shoot in that period or lose the ball.

Chase was a magnificent interview subject. He understood my ambition and sensed that I admired his work.

"I think hockey's the easiest game to broadcast," he told me that day. "It's almost continuous action. You don't have to wait for players to unpile, like in football, or wait between pitches, like you do in baseball, or wait through the timeouts of basketball."

After the interview was completed, he took time to create a reel-to-reel transfer of my favorite Chase moment—his call of a playoff game–tying goal at the horn by Komets center Len Thornson.

When I reached the parking lot, I doubled back to the reception desk and asked to see him again. I had forgotten that I had brought along a photograph I had cut out of a Komets program. When he came out to the front lobby, I asked him to sign it for me. He graciously obliged.

I was on top of the world that day, but I knew even then the odds were stacked against me as far as my aspirations to be a hockey play-by-play announcer were concerned.

If you graduate with a degree in teaching, you enter a job market that includes 50 states and countless schools and opportunities. If you graduate with a degree in engineering, you will be looking at a long list of companies that need your abilities.

My situation was far different. When I graduated from Manchester in 1968 dreaming of a hockey job, I looked at a professional hockey landscape that included 12 NHL teams, seven IHL teams, and eight American Hockey League teams as my primary potential employers. And how many of those jobs were turning over that year? Probably no more than two or three. Other pro teams did exist, but not many.

I decided to go straight to graduate school at Miami (Ohio) University, because I had no television experience and Miami offered a one-year master's program in radio and television.

The following spring, armed with more television experience, I mailed tapes of the "broadcasts" I created from the stands at the Coliseum to all minor league hockey teams. What came back was rejection letter after rejection letter.

I needed a job and, because I had a master's degree, I was able to find one at Geneva College in Beaver College, Pennsylvania.

Trying to keep at least one foot in the hockey world, I called the *Beaver County Times* and offered to cover the Pittsburgh Penguins for free in exchange for the newspaper's assistance in securing a press pass for the season.

Terry Schiffhauer, the cordial young Penguins public relations director, shepherded me through my first Penguins press day. The experience only furthered my desire to become a hockey broadcaster.

Goalie Les Binkley was the first NHL player I ever interviewed, and he talked about the challenges of experimenting with a mask in training camp. Some goalies were still reluctant to use them in that era.

I asked Bryan Hextall which NHL arena he considered the toughest to play in. Without hesitation, he said it was the Boston Garden.

"I was standing at center ice in Boston Garden before the game. They were making a presentation to [Bobby] Orr, and, out of the stands, over my shoulder comes a huge lock like you'd put on the front of a garage. It just missed me, hit the ice, and cracked it right through to the concrete," Hextall said.

In the spring of 1971, I sent out more tapes and got more rejections. At that point, I was wondering whether my future might be in college teaching.

My father, always skeptical that I could make a career in broadcasting, suggested that the best time to complete my dissertation was right then, when I was young and had no family. He told me how difficult it was to earn his master's degree while he was married with two children.

I applied for doctoral assistantship (tuition-free) at the University of Michigan and Bowling Green because they had stations that carried the schools' hockey games.

Bowling Green became my top choice when Terry Shaw (real name Gottschalk), the program director of WBGU-FM, told me that the student play-by-play guy had graduated.

Shaw, who was the main play-by-play announcer for football, basketball, and hockey, said I could be the second-period play-by-play guy and color analyst if I came there. A former player, Bob Schmidt, was also an analyst.

I was sold.

My first official hockey broadcast—not counting the Fort Wayne practice broadcasts—was a Bowling Green game against Ryerson College, a Canadian school, in the fall of 1971.

Understandably, I didn't sleep well the night before the game. I don't remember much about my second period other than that Shaw was polite and complimentary. Bob was as well. And Bowling Green won the game.

Another memorable game was one that I was forbidden from broadcasting. Our Central Collegiate Hockey Association rivals, the Ohio State Buckeyes, said their rink was too small to accommodate a table needed to set up our equipment.

None of that made sense to us, but we had no standing to argue.

By agreement, I was allowed into the rink manager's office to phone in reports (by placing a collect call) twice per period.

My solace was that after the game I was able to report that Rich Nagai had scored in overtime to beat the Buckeyes.

The Bowling Green experience was close to perfect. A woman named Gladys French and her husband, nicknamed "Yogi," rented me a room in their basement for a reasonable price. It had a bunk bed, and you shared a kitchen and bathroom with fellow basement dwellers. One of those was a Penguins fan named Bob Dickinson, who made the experience more enjoyable. Good guy.

The Bowling Green Falcons team included Ted Sator, a future NHL coach, and the goalie was Don Boyd, who ended up as a prominent Canadian junior coach. They were coached by Jack Vivian, who would coach briefly in the World Hockey Association. Jack ended up being a good friend.

During the 1971–72 and 1972–73 seasons, I broadcast 18 home games, plus two playoff games. That's a total of 40 periods over two seasons. I finally had a legitimate demo to send out. I sent one to the Port Huron Flags and received a call from John Wismer, the team's original owner. He wanted to talk to me. He said he already had my résumé, which had included the tapes I made from the Fort Wayne stands.

I don't know if he listened to either tape, but he wanted to talk to me about a job. I couldn't drive to Port Huron fast enough.

CAPTURE THE FLAGS

As I sat nervously in radio station owner John Wismer's office in 1973 discussing the possibility of landing my first professional hockey broadcasting job, I felt like a canary bargaining with an alley cat.

Chances were good that I would be eaten alive in these negotiations.

"Big John" was a self-assured, shrewd businessman, a pillar in the Port Huron, Michigan, community of 35,000 people. I was a man with expansive dreams and ambition but limited leverage and experience. One of my drawers housed a pile of rejection letters from teams all around the country.

Wismer, born and raised in Port Huron, surrendered a good job in sales with the Beech-Nut gum company in the 1940s to buy the failing WHLS radio station. His brother, Harry Wismer, had owned the New York Titans (turned Jets), one of the original American Football League teams.

In his first week of ownership, Wismer went knocking on doors throughout the community and collected every bad debt owed to WHLS. He made it clear his radio station would be managed far differently than it had been in the past. It wasn't charity. It was business. In a short period of time, he built WHLS into a source of pride for Port Huron.

Wismer also brought the International Hockey League's Port Huron Flags to the city in 1962. This wasn't business. This was ol' John's heart. He loved hockey and owning a team. He owned the Flags for nine years, losing a bundle of money, before selling them to the city for $1.

But he kept the team's broadcasting rights for his radio station, and that's why in 1973 I was sitting across his enormous desk with a bundle of broadcast tapes and written notes that I hoped would persuade him I was the man for the job. The second I met him, the interview went in an unexpected direction.

"Hello, Michael," he said. "So, how much is this going to cost me?"

Panic engulfed me as I realized that my ability to claim this position wasn't coming down to my hockey expertise, or how I sounded on the air, but rather how much money I wanted in my pocket. I had prepared myself for many questions he might ask, but not the one about how much money I should earn.

Shocked by his straightforward approach, I pretended to compute some financial calculations on the papers on my lap. What I was trying to do was determine the line between making myself a non-candidate and a livable wage.

"One hundred and 60 dollars a week," I blurted out.

"That will be fine," Wismer said.

Instantly, I knew I had been no match for Wismer as a negotiator. He had purposely put me on the spot, accurately projecting that I would come in lower, rather than higher.

Before then, I had been broadcasting Bowling Green State University college hockey games. After accepting the Port Huron job, I called Falcons coach Jack Vivian to tell him the news.

"Congratulations," he said. "But what are you making?"

"Eighty-three hundred dollars a year," I said, sheepishly.

I should have added I also would receive $7 a day for meal money for trips over 200 miles and $3 for trips under 200.

"Holy cow," Vivian said. "You're working for nothing."

Jack's wife grabbed the phone to congratulate me and give me ammunition to use in the defense of my poor negotiation skills. "Just ask Jack how much he made in his first coaching job," she said, laughing.

That day, Wismer probably felt as if he was the winner because I agreed to work for the paltry sum of $8,320 per year. But maybe the joke was on John, because I would have done that job for nothing.

As I often say, the best benefit of my job is that I can watch hockey games for free. I understood that back then as much as I do today.

I FOUND A NICE ROOM in town with a landlord named Dorothy Myers, for $35 per week. That included a lovely Sunday brunch. I made sure to ask Dorothy if she needed anything from the grocery store on the way home from church.

Broadcasting Port Huron games turned out to be as captivating as I had hoped. Minor league hockey, especially in the 1970s, seemed more important than it truly was.

Not everyone in Port Huron followed the team, but everyone was aware of its presence. Port Huron general manager Morris Snider made sure that was true, promoting the team with the enthusiasm of a carnival barker.

Step right up and see the greatest show in town!

It was exhilarating to show up at the rink on a game day. As soon as the doors opened, you could sense the buzz in the crowd, even if there were only 1,400 in attendance. It was the same feeling that I had when I attended Komets games as a child.

Unquestionably, some fans in that era came to games with the anticipation, or expectation, that fighting or brawling would occur. Chaos and mayhem were part of the IHL's lure in those days. In 1973–74, Gord Malinoski led the IHL with 333 penalty minutes, and there were a dozen other players who were just as likely to fight as he was.

Sometimes newspaper reporters would fan flames with stories about the rivalries between teams and players. General managers and coaches would fuel newspaper stories with inflammatory comments, designed specifically to entice more people to move through the turnstiles.

Regular fans didn't need newspaper stories to keep them apprised of the importance of each game. In every IHL city, regular fans understood the history, grudges, and personalities.

If there was a fight on the ice, regulars could pinpoint the game three seasons before that had prompted this battle. The IHL had a gladiatorial tone, and I enjoyed every minute I was in the broadcast booth.

Although I am rightfully associated with the Port Huron Flags organization, my first season as a professional broadcaster was spent as the voice of the renamed Port Huron Wings. We were considered the lowest-level farm team of the Detroit Red Wings.

This was a crazy time in the professional hockey world because the World Hockey Association had opened for business the previous season.

NHL superstar Bobby Hull, the league's reigning goal-scoring king, had been presented with a $1 million check on the steps of Winnipeg's city hall. After a year of working for the Red Wings in a figurehead role, the recently retired great Gordie Howe had un-retired to sign a contract to play with sons Mark and Marty Howe and the Houston Aeros.

The WHA had ambitious plans for growth and was raiding the NHL and American Hockey League for players.

The trickle-down effect reached all the way down to Port Huron. Minor league teams were scrambling for players, which was why Snider was happy to reach an affiliation agreement with the Red Wings.

On the day I arrived in Port Huron, new Red Wings general manager Ned Harkness had promised Snider and coach Bob McCammon that the Red Wings could loan 14 players to the Port Huron team.

Minor league general managers always worked hard to sell tickets, and it would certainly help to point out that future Red Wings would be on the team.

The only problem with the plan was Red Wings owner Bruce Norris, a man who enjoyed spending time in England. One of his brainstorms had produced a plan to place a professional hockey team in London, even though the country had no real history in the sport. The plan was for the London Lions to play Europe's national teams. Norris believed he was opening a gateway to a fresh European market.

Because Norris didn't want to disrupt the competitiveness of the Red Wings' top farm team in Virginia, his plan was to stock the London franchise with the players promised to Port Huron. It meant that the Port Huron Wings would be given the leftovers of leftovers of leftovers. The rosters of the Red Wings, London Lions, and Virginia Wings would be filled before Port Huron's needs were addressed.

Despite the change in plans, I was full of optimism and energy when the Detroit Red Wings brought 65 players to Port Huron's McMorran Arena for training camp.

It didn't matter to me who would be on the roster, or how much opportunity the team would have for success. I was just thrilled to have a job in the world of professional hockey.

When Red Wings announcer and former Port Huron announcer Len Hardman handed me the team's roster, I was as riveted and delighted to read the list as a child would be surveying toys in a Sears, Roebuck, & Co. catalog.

"Thought you might like to look over the guys," Hardman had said.

A few minutes later, as I stood next to the rink working to place names with faces, Hardman sheepishly walked up and asked for the roster back.

"Ned Harkness doesn't want you to have it. I don't know why," Hardman said.

Later in the day, Snider explained that Harkness was concerned about my friendship with Jack Vivian, who had just left Bowling Green to become general manager of the WHA's Cleveland Crusaders.

"The WHA is signing players right off the ice in NHL camps. Ned was concerned you were reporting in to [Vivian]," Hardman said.

Imagine my uneasiness. Two months into my job, and I'm suspected of being a corporate spy.

Obviously, nothing more ever came of this. And to be honest, the Port Huron franchise didn't receive much benefit from its association with the Red Wings. When our IHL training camp opened the following week, Tommy Newman was the only player the NHL franchise loaned to Port Huron.

Snider signed some former Port Huron players who were still living in the area, such as Ray Germain, Billy Watt, and Danny Newman. The remaining players were players cut by other IHL teams.

It was probably obvious to everyone in the IHL that the Port Huron Wings were destined for a losing season. But it never crossed my mind that we would be a bad team. Ignorance was bliss. At that point, I was too excited to be a broadcaster and too naïve as a talent evaluator to appreciate how poorly this team might play.

My focus was soaking up the atmosphere that came with being an IHL broadcaster. The thrill of riding the bus to games wore off, but I have vivid memories of the delight I felt taking the two-hour bus ride to Toledo, Ohio, for my first Port Huron Wings broadcast.

The team was playing the Toledo Hornets in the old Toledo Sports Arena. The building was located on the waterfront, on the seedy side of the city, but I was just as excited as I would have been if my first game was on the Las Vegas strip.

I was a professional play-by-play broadcaster. What did I care where we played? I proudly walked into the tired old rink lugging my enormous red suitcase embossed with the Red Wings logo and painted with the WHLS call letters. Inside I carried a 6"x6" homemade mixer box, designed for two microphones. I had a lavalier microphone. It was a two-inch microphone attached to a coat hanger that was looped to go around my neck. It held the microphone in place to allow me to have my hands free to write on my scorecard. It came with a hard-shell plastic headset to allow me to hear myself when I spoke. Station engineer Marc Carmen had put my equipment together.

As primitive as the equipment may seem now, I was thankful to have it back then. I would have shouted play-by-play through a megaphone if that was the only way I could broadcast hockey games.

My adrenaline was flowing for the first game. A Port Huron vs. Toledo game had built-in hostility. A bar, featuring hard liquor, was located just inside the turnstiles. Some fans were well lubricated by game time. Toledo has been called the glass capital of North America, making it ironic that the Toledo Sports Arena had no Plexiglas. Wire screens were attached to the boards, making it far easier for Toledo fans to launch projectiles and insults at opposing players.

It was a dangerous journey for opposing players to travel from the visiting dressing room to the ice. Players had to walk across a concourse, down a hallway, past some beer stands, and then climb a short set of stairs with fans walking next to them. Then they walked down three rows to the ice.

The Hornets stationed uniformed policemen at the front of the 18-player parade and another at the back to keep the peace. But it didn't always work. Occasionally, skirmishes between players and drunken fans would erupt. The worst ones occurred at the end of the second intermission when patrons' alcohol levels were at their highest.

This was McCammon's first game as Port Huron's coach, but he had been visiting Toledo for 11 seasons as an All-Star player.

McCammon told me later that he had playfully asked the police officer near the bench whether he ever had trouble with crowd control.

Not sensing that the question was a joke, the policeman said in a serious tone: "Well, there's one guy in the last row who has been sling-shooting bullets at the visitors' bench."

He added: "We know he's doing it, but we just can't catch him."

McCammon thought he had heard it all about the Toledo Sports Arena until he heard that story.

Although the game was 45 years ago, I remember many of the details, including that one of the returning players, left wing Dale Dolmage, rocketed a "left-circle whistler" over the "lightning-like" glove hand of Glenn Ramsay for the game-winner in a 6–5 Port Huron victory.

The Wings were 1–0 after Game 1, and that was probably the best day of their season. Port Huron finished with the league's worst record (29–44–3) in 1973–74.

Flint Generals announcer Carl Robertson said, "McCammon should be coach of the year just for getting through the season with that group."

The team's pile of losses didn't prevent me from enjoying my first professional season as a broadcaster. I learned much about the sport from McCammon, who had befriended me on my first day on the job. Snider treated me with unwavering respect.

Unquestionably, I had some memorable moments, like the on-ice wedding between periods at the Des Moines Capitols game against Port Huron on December 14, 1973.

"It won't change much," Capitols public relations director/broadcaster Paul Viglianti told me. "Your team won't stay on the ice, but our team will. It will only lengthen the intermission by 10 minutes."

The wedding made perfect sense from a promotional standpoint. Ron Jensen, president of the Capitols' fan club, was marrying club member Lois Riley. Why not get married on the ice at a Des Moines game?

The team asked for a Friday night nuptial, because Friday was always a difficult attendance night for the Capitols. Friday night was girls high school basketball night at Veterans Memorial Stadium.

"Girls basketball will draw 10,000 there on a Friday night and we usually get 1,500," Viglianti said. "We are hoping to get 1,800, maybe more, because of the wedding."

McCammon agreed to the plan. His team would leave the ice after the first period and coach Danny Belisle and the Capitols players, including Steve Coates, who would go on to play in the NHL and become a Philadelphia Flyers broadcaster, would remain on the ice for the ceremony.

During the first period, the wedding preparations started to go awry when Belisle, angered over one of referee Ron Fournier's calls, kicked at the bench and ended up booting Lois Riley's flower bouquet. Unbeknownst to Belisle, the flowers had been stored under the bench for safe keeping.

That hilarious moment was an omen of other calamities to come.

Preparing to cover the extra 10 minutes of the intermission, I had taped what I considered a forgettable interview with the groom, Ron Jensen.

Rookie interviewer with a nervous subject produced a poor feature. My questions were too typical, and his answers were too short.

But needing to fill 10 extra minutes, we used the interview after WHLS personality Ron Dzwonkowski provided a news brief from the Port Huron studio.

Once we dispensed with the filler material, I came back on the air and set the scene for the wedding. I described the ambiance. A white mat was rolled out along the red line at center ice. Out walked the minister and the groom.

The radiant bride walked out on a separate white mat stretching from the corner of the rink to center ice.

The Des Moines players, all heavily perspiring from the first period, were lined up on both sides of the long, white mat. As the bride walked out to center ice, the players raised their sticks, with blades touching, to form an arch for her to walk under.

When you consider the smell of the sweaty players and the odor of beer that is always present at hockey games, the bride undoubtedly had to be thinking, "This sure doesn't smell like a church."

At first, the plan was working. The minister provided an appropriate marital message over the public-address system. Vows were exchanged. Rings were slid onto fingers. Kisses were planted. The happy couple walked out under the hockey stick arch.

That's when it began to unravel. The expected crowd of 1,800 turned out to be 2,787. The fans all had stayed in their seats to view the wedding, and they wanted to be active participants in the ceremony.

In the Midwest, in 1973, it was customary to shower a newly married couple with rice. Guests were often supplied with a small amount of rice wrapped up in a decorative doily.

No rice was available that night at the Oak Creek Ice Arena. But most fans were holding programs, popcorn, cups of beer, and other throwable objects.

And each of those items started flying over the wire screen as the fans found a way to salute the couple and preserve the wedding tradition.

Because I was all out of commercials, I just started doing play-by-play on what was occurring on the ice: "And a man in the second row, near the blue line, just hurled his…"

When the fans were done celebrating the wedding, the arena's two-man maintenance department was ankle-deep in debris. This necessitated detaching the nets and pushing them around like rakes to scoop up the bigger pieces.

Instead of filling 10 extra minutes, I had to fill 45 extra minutes. That's how long it took to restore the ice to a playable condition. It is what I call "guts broadcasting." Nothing to describe, just filling time with stories, insights, perspectives, and predictions. Anything short of saying hello to your mother is acceptable.

Maybe that was the night I earned my stripes as a broadcaster. If you can fill 45 extra minutes, you can handle almost anything that comes up.

The Port Huron Wings won that game 5–3, but the Capitols went on to enjoy a memorable season, winning the Turner Cup championship. A funny side note is the organization celebrated the title by retiring the numbers of everyone who played on that championship team. The following season, the lowest number that could appear on a Des Moines player's back was 21.

Snider also made changes to his franchise. After the Red Wings announced they were putting their own IHL farm team in Kalamazoo, Michigan, Snider made a deal to become an affiliate with the NHL expansion Kansas City Scouts.

The Scouts were run by former Red Wings great Sid Abel, who was one of Snider's buddies. They were close enough friends that Abel decided to hold his training camp in Port Huron.

Wismer and Snider also got together and made two more decisions. The first was that the Port Huron team was going to be renamed the Flags. Second, I was going to be given the part-time job as the team's public relations director.

I now had two half-time jobs that required about 80 hours per week during the winter. I never complained about any of it, and Snider found a way to give me a $20 per week raise. I immediately told Dorothy she would share in my good fortune with a raise to $40 a week for the room.

THE OTHER NEWS THAT OFF-SEASON was that I'd found a girlfriend.

One night, Bob McCammon and his wife, Marie, invited me to their home on Erie Street. Little Joey and Susie, their two children, were there. It was an enjoyable evening.

At one point, when the hockey talk died down for moment, Marie drove a velvet bulldozer into the lull of the conversation.

"So," Marie said, "do you have a girlfriend?"

"Marie!" Bob interrupted. "Leave him alone. Look at him, he's happy!"

To be honest, I had not been looking for a girlfriend because my first year in Port Huron was all about my job.

Ignoring her husband's request, Marie slipped me the number of a young woman named Joyce Ann Sult, who attended the same church that Marie did.

Unrelated to that event, my church was planning a party for young singles. My job was to help invite people. I noticed that Joyce was on the list. She wasn't on my list to call, but someone else called her and she accepted the invitation. I was going to meet her before I decided whether to ask her out.

Years later, I would learn she attended the party despite feeling "queasy" from "being in the sun all day."

What I discovered that night was that she was a nice person, well-spoken, with beautiful blue eyes and a cheerful laugh. She also had a good job as an accounts payable overseer at Beard Campbell, a wholesale hardware company. The Campbell family later spawned an NHL goalie named Jack Campbell.

It took me six weeks to ask her on a date. We were supposed to see *Dr. Zhivago*, starring Omar Sharif and Julie Christie. It's a four-hour epic, a tragic love story with the Russian Revolution serving for the backdrop.

Unfortunately, I got lost and we were too late to make the starting time of that picture and ended up driving to nearby Marysville, Michigan, to see *Butch Cassidy and the Sundance Kid*, starring Paul Newman and Robert Redford. It's a western blending drama with humor, and a much better first-date movie.

The movie was followed by a late dinner at Big Boy, which included their famous hot fudge cake for dessert. Seemed like a perfect first date.

As we walked out of Big Boy, she spied two newspaper boxes. She pounded the coin return nob as we walked past them.

"Occasionally, a quarter comes out," Joyce said.

I made a note that my potential new girlfriend probably liked slot machines.

Another Joyce attribute that added to her attractiveness was that she was tolerant of my ambition. She knew I wanted to leave Port Huron and yet she didn't flinch, even though she had no desire to ever leave. Her job, her mother and stepfather, and her twin brother and his wife were all in the area.

My desire to leave was rooted in my hope to someday be an NHL broadcaster. But I also understood that the Port Huron team didn't afford me job security because the team's future was always in doubt. The hockey team was a political football. At some point, the city was going to punt it.

Many citizens were asking the question about why the city was willing to accept $300,000 in losses just to have a tenant in McMorran Arena.

It was a fair and reasonable question.

As much as I appreciated my Port Huron experience, I was already thinking about my next stop. With Snider's blessing, I applied for the Pittsburgh Penguins' radio job on the 50,000-watt KDKA. Snider even placed a call to Penguins general manager Jack Button on my behalf.

An old friend, Terry Schiffhauer, was part of the decision-making group. "You're right in there," he told me.

I made it to the final three but the job went to Mike Lange, who had been broadcasting Phoenix Roadrunners games in the Western Hockey League.

It was no shame to lose out to Lange, who became a Pittsburgh legend with his unique play-by-play style, which included his signature "Elvis has just left the building" call. The Penguins made the right choice.

Meanwhile, back in Michigan, the Port Huron Flags were a rejuvenated organization, thanks to a new season ticket program. We offered the same seat for 40 games for $99. Or, for the same price, a fan could receive 40 coupons which could be exchanged at the box office for tickets for any game. In other words, you could secure 40 tickets for one game if that was your need.

Fans liked the new plan, and we were comfortable that we would always be able to accommodate ticket requests. We had averaged 1,410 fans per game in 1973–74, and our capacity was 3,300. We never came close to that.

I wanted to help with the marketing and I had an idea, stolen from the Philadelphia Flyers. Could we hire famed entertainer Kate Smith to sing "God Bless America" at the 1974–75 home opener? Her presence had been a major story during the Flyers' recent march to the Stanley Cup championship.

The Flyers provided me with her agent's number. I explained where Port Huron was located and that all expenses would be paid if Ms. Smith would lend her voice to the Flags' opener.

"It'll cost you $10,000, plus expenses," the agent said.

"Thanks," I said.

I took the details to Snider and received the expected answer.

"When you are losing $300,000 a year on an operation, you don't spend $10,000 for 90 seconds," he said.

Understood.

Snider played hardball when it came to negotiations. This was an era when players didn't have agents, and contracts were heavily weighted toward management's benefit. They had to be for the Flags to stay in business. At least, that's the way Snider portrayed his position to players.

"I'm responsible to the city manager," Snider would say. "I'd love to give you what you want, but I came to the ballpark with a basket full of balls. It's 4:00 and the basket is almost empty. Here's what I can pay you."

Snider could also make you feel like he was being overly generous with his offer, like he once did with Claude Julien, the same Julien who now coaches the Montreal Canadiens. Julien played one season with the Port Huron Flags in 1980–81.

"I normally pay rookie defensemen $250," Snider told him. "But I like you, so you get $300."

Julien told me later that he couldn't help but accept with a pitch like that.

No matter how tight Snider was with player contracts, the Flags still lost money. But in 1974–75, my second season in Port Huron, we showed improvement on and off the ice. The Flags were 35–38–3. We lost to coach Moose Lallo's Muskegon Mohawks in the first round of the playoffs. Maybe more importantly, the Flags raised their average attendance from 1,465 to 1,610.

The Flags were still hemorrhaging red ink, but the situation was improving.

In 1975–76, it felt as if the Flags were turning the corner, particularly after Detroit Lions chaplain Lloyd Livingston was brought in as a motivational speaker to address the Flags in November.

Livingston wasn't there to discuss God or religion, although he would have been happy to have that conversation if a player had asked.

The Flags were about to play in Saginaw, a place where they had never been victorious. It was Livingston's job to infuse self-confidence into players who couldn't find any when they traveled the 104 miles from Port Huron to the Saginaw Civic Center.

Near the end of his talk, Livingston asked players to think about playing in Saginaw on December 5.

Earlier in the season, the Flags had already been beaten by Saginaw 6–4. But Livingston asked Port Huron players to think about looking up at the scoreboard at the next game and seeing Port Huron beating the Gears.

Livingston's talk was self-actualization at its finest.

"You will say, 'We're ahead of Saginaw,'" Livingston said. "It will be with a minute to go, and you will trust each other because of all you have been through. You will say, 'We are going to beat Saginaw.' Then when the horn sounds, you'll be experiencing the greatest feeling in sports. Exhausted but victorious."

That's exactly what happened. The Flags defeated the Gears 7–3 in Saginaw in their next meeting. It was a significant confidence boost for the Flags. That win inspired the team to a higher level of play—they won seven of nine during a surge that started in Saginaw.

The Gears (43–26–9) finished as the North Division champions and the Flags (36–31–11) finished second. But the win in Saginaw had changed the rivalry. Livingston's speech had made the Flags realize they had the ability to slay the dragon in the dragon's lair. They could win in Saginaw.

By sweeping the Flint Generals in the opening round of playoffs, the Flags earned the right to play Saginaw in the second round.

Livingston was brought in again to address the team, to provide the right words, to push the right buttons, to coax the highest level of performance out of the Flags.

As you might expect, the best-of-seven series went the distance, meaning the deciding game would be played in Saginaw.

This game didn't use a regular IHL referee. It was officiated by an NHL import. And in the opening three minutes of the game, Port Huron forward Bill Watt found himself in a fight with a Saginaw player in the faceoff circle. It was an unnecessary battle, particularly given the importance of the game.

Port Huron's leading scorer Len Fontaine was playing alongside Watt, and he joined the fray to help his teammate. Maybe a regular IHL referee would have deemed it "entrapment" on the Gears' part because Fontaine and Watt were valuable to Port Huron.

The NHL referee ejected Fontaine and Watt. In an instant, the Flags' chances of winning this game had been dramatically undermined.

Fontaine was a 53-goal scorer that season, and Watt had netted 24. That was 77 goals stripped from the Port Huron team. Plus, Fontaine was the team's most seasoned and accomplished player. He was the team's go-to performer. The season before he had played against Hull and Howe in the World Hockey Association.

Incensed over the loss of two premium players, Snider stormed out of the arena. He had high blood pressure, and he felt it would be better for his health if didn't watch his team play without those two players.

IHL commissioner Bill Beagan chased Snider and found him pacing in the parking lot. Beagan and Snider were friends, and Beagan said afterward he feared Snider might suffer a heart attack.

What Snider didn't see was his team pulling together and playing one of its best games of the season. The Flags claimed a 2–0 lead, saw it cut in half in the third period, and then hung on for a 3–1 triumph. Defenseman Charlie Shaw, a Detroit Red Wings draft pick, scored the insurance goal against Mario Lessard, who would end up playing in the NHL.

In the jubilant Flags dressing room, players chanted "Lloyd, Lloyd, Lloyd" in recognition of Livingston's contributions to their reaching the Turner Cup Final. He had unlocked their minds, removed doubts, and persuaded them to believe in themselves. Livingston's words were as important as a few clutch saves.

In the IHL final, the Flags were swept by the Dayton Gems. The Gems had been coached by Tommy McVie, who had just been promoted to the Washington Capitals. Legendary IHL tough guy Ivan Prediger was brought as a replacement, or as he called it "to open and close the bench gate." But the general perception was the Flags had enjoyed a memorable season. They looked like a team on the rise. Average attendance had risen from 1,450 to 1,610 to 1,751 in my first three seasons in Port Huron.

I was comfortable with the way my career was progressing. Getting close to the job in Pittsburgh had bolstered my confidence. I still loved my job in Port Huron. I had a steady girlfriend who supported my desire to move elsewhere, even though she wanted to stay in Port Huron. I had a great life.

My career ambitions were of secondary importance to the reality that Port Huron was in danger of losing its talented coach. McCammon was viewed around the hockey world as someone with the potential to become an NHL coach.

What I didn't understand at the time was that our futures would be tied together.

TOO MANY
SUE HAMILTONS

When the door opened for Port Huron Flags coach Bob McCammon to take his considerable talent to a higher level in 1977, I managed to squeeze through with him.

The NHL's Philadelphia Flyers, two years removed from winning back-to-back Stanley Cup championships, had decided to bankroll a new American Hockey League affiliate in Portland, Maine. Flyers general manager Keith Allen dialed up his friend Ken Ullyot, then GM of the Fort Wayne Komets, to ask for a recommendation for a coach to hire.

At least, that's the story that was told around the IHL back then.

Allen wanted a teaching coach who could develop young players for Flyers coach Fred Shero.

Ullyot, who had played with Allen in Saskatchewan in 1945–46, told him that McCammon might be the man he was seeking. Although McCammon had missed the playoffs the previous season in Port Huron, he had already established his credentials as a coach who knew how to improve players and teams.

In 1975–76, McCammon had coached a ham-and-eggs, low-budget Port Huron team all the way to the Turner Cup Final. When Port Huron upset Saginaw in Game 7, McCammon and Snider found a congratulatory message on the TWX machine from the already-eliminated Fort Wayne Komets.

McCammon always lived up to his nickname, "Cagey." Ullyot had witnessed enough of McCammon's tricks to feel confident he was recommending a capable man. A year earlier, McCammon had pulled his goalie and scored a tying goal by defenseman Larry Klewchuk with one second left in regulation against Fort Wayne. Then, Alex Kogler had scored in overtime to beat the Komets in Fort Wayne.

In many ways, McCammon was ahead of his time, particularly when it came time to pull his goalie in the closing minutes.

When the Flags were trailing 5–2 one night in a game in Port Huron, McCammon pulled his goalie with six minutes remaining. That was not what coaches did in the 1970s. Fort Wayne fans were already filing out of the building, but they returned to their seats, expecting to be rewarded for their loyalty with empty-net goals.

But that didn't happen. Instead, the Flags scored quickly and then netted another after the ensuing faceoff. Now it was a one-goal game. The Flags pressed, but only a defenseman's block on a Len Fontaine shot in the closing seconds prevented the Flags from tying the score. The gears were always turning when McCammon was behind the bench.

It was McCammon who planted the idea that it might be possible for me to accompany him to this new team in Maine.

"You should put in an application for the announcing job," McCammon told me that spring.

That thought created instant excitement. As an NHL affiliate, Maine would be one step away from the NHL for both the players and me.

I did my own investigation, which meant I called the Flyers, and uncovered that Gil Stein would be hiring the broadcaster. If the name sounds familiar, it's because this was the same Gil Stein who eventually would rise to the rank of NHL president in 1992. He was the last president before Gary Bettman was hired as the commissioner.

Immediately, I called and left a message for Stein, asking for a callback. After a week passed, I called again. I became a regular, and Stein's secretary always told me she was giving Stein the message.

I assumed that Stein always leafed through his pink message slips and I hoped the frequency of my name appearing in that stack would work in my favor. Leaving a message was like buying tiny billboard advertising. I'm confident he was receiving 30 or more messages every day. But my hope was that this form of advertising would result in Stein remembering my name.

It must have worked because a month after I began leaving messages, in June 1977, I received a call from his secretary.

"Mr. Stein wants you to know that he'll be interviewing all of the broadcasting and marketing candidates next week," she said. "We cannot pay any expenses, but if you would like to come to Portland, he will allot you 15 minutes."

I had plenty of support in Port Huron to land the job in Maine, and not just from McCammon. Wismer and team general manager Morris Snider were rooting for me to move on because we all understood that the Flags' future in Port Huron was season-to-season.

Even after the Flags had reached the Turner Cup Final, their return the following season was in question. With more wins came higher attendance, but the cost of operating a pro team in a heavily industrialized state such as Michigan was much higher than in other states because of disability insurance payments.

At that time, the Flags' disability insurance cost four times what the Fort Wayne Komets paid in the heavily agricultural state of Indiana. Wismer and three of his well-to-do friends contributed $10,000 each the previous summer to pay for the insurance. It was impossible to know how much longer their generosity would continue.

It was clear to most of us that the Flags were on borrowed time.

Once I knew I had a scheduled interview, I consulted with friends about how to win the job, particularly Ted Findley, who was the energetic and innovative editor of the *Port Huron Times Herald* newspaper. I liked Ted and respected his insights on how life worked. He would occasionally have lunch with McCammon and me. We'd swap stories and laugh a great deal. I appreciated that he would spend his wisdom on two hockey guys.

"I need some advice," I told Findley. "God only knows how long the team will remain here and Bob just told me of a new franchise in the American Hockey League for the Philadelphia Flyers. They have been to the final three straight years, won the Stanley Cup twice, and are loaded with dough. I am going to get 15 minutes with the Flyers president next week. What do I do?"

Without pausing for even a moment, Findley offered a plan.

"Get all the information on Portland you can get," Findley said. "Then you walk in with more than you'll be able to discuss in 15 minutes. Just point out to him, this is my plan for you to look over. It includes a demographic study on the marketplace, what I would do if I were hired to be your PR man and broadcaster, and a résumé and audition tape."

I had long ago mailed Stein a tape of one of my broadcasts. But the rest of the plan seemed terrific.

When I showed up at the team's temporary office in Portland, Ed Anderson, the future team president, was sitting in a room with his hands wrapped around a sizeable stack of postcards. Fans had been asked to use postcards to send in their votes for what the team nickname should be.

Anderson was extremely busy that day tabulating the voting results with Kara Lynn Dunn, who had been hired as a public relations assistant.

As Anderson read the cards, Dunn was making a mark on a sheet of paper to keep a running tally. That mission was probably more pressing, and more important, than talking to me.

But Anderson would later tell me, "I remember it seemed like you were really glad to be there."

That was the truth. I was nervous but enjoyed some confidence, helped by the fact that I had taken a Dale Carnegie course the previous winter.

In the first week, I won the Dale Carnegie ballpoint pen for my speech. Then I hit a dry spell. I didn't feel like any of my speeches were well received. One night, after class, I asked instructor Hank Knight for a critique.

"I don't know how to say this," he said, "except to say, it's like you are talking down to us."

Those words packed a heavy punch. Is that how I was coming across? As a know-it-all or a snob?

But I took the criticism to heart. I took my Carnegie principles with me when I went to interview. One of those principles is: "There is no sweeter sound to any person than the sound of their own name." I started jotting down the names of people I met. Instead of concentrating on what I wanted to say, I tried to sense what was important to each person I met.

Thanks to Findley's advice, I felt prepared to be one of the 40 candidates for the broadcasting/public relations job in Maine. I was invited into Stein's office and gave him my folder of material, briefly explaining I was leaving it with him for his review. I had a brief—emphasis on brief—presentation not about what I wanted, but how I thought I could help Maine's new team.

My 15 minutes expanded to 40. I thought the interview went well. As I was leaving, Stein told me he had many more candidates to speak with and "you will be notified of my decision."

Although I flew into Portland that morning and flew out that afternoon, in two cab rides from the Portland Jetport to the offices and back, I had seen enough of the landscape and the community to have a sense this was going to be great.

I couldn't wait to call McCammon from the Portland Jetport.

"This place is going to be like Saginaw," I said, the highest compliment I could pay a franchise that could be turned into great success. "You'd love it out here. Lots of sea air, smaller community, interesting people, and no previous experience with hockey. Given the amount of money the Flyers have and their willingness to promote it, you'd love it."

A few days after my calls, McCammon informed me that he had been hired by the Maine franchise.

Wismer authorized me to fly to Portland to cover his press conference for our radio station. Secretly, Wismer just wanted Stein to see me in action as a reporter. He was trying to help me land this job.

From the time the airliner hit the ground, my wheels started moving. I interviewed McCammon, Keith Allen, who was doing the hiring, and Stein. I was aggressive and visible.

After the press conference, Stein called me into his office.

"Mike, I just want to share with you the outcome of the announcer interviews," he said professionally. There was no warmth in his voice.

Though Stein was an attorney of the highest order, he was unable to hide his feelings. I knew from the phrasing of his first sentence that I wasn't being offered the job.

"I forwarded all the tapes to Harlan Singer, our broadcast producer," Stein said. "And he said, while your tape was head and shoulders above all the others, there was one other that was head and shoulders above you. I am sorry, but you finished second."

Although I was disappointed and a little shocked, I responded the way Dale Carnegie and Ted Findley would have wanted.

"Thank you for your consideration," I said, making eye contact. "Might I be able to speak with Mr. Singer and see if there is an area where I might improve so that next time, I might be chosen?"

Immediately, Stein reached for his phone and dialed. Singer answered on the other end. Stein relayed both ends of our conversation, that I "was being a big boy about this," and that I wanted his advice. He handed me the phone.

"I cannot put a finger on it," he said. "It's simply a question of style. I just liked his style better than yours. In the end it's just what I preferred. Another audition, another judge besides me, and you might have come out on top."

I thanked him and flew home. There was one upside. By now, plans were going forward for at least one more Flags season. I could spend another year in familiar surroundings and in Joyce's company.

Joyce and I had never made plans beyond dating. I had made it clear that my hope was to climb the career ladder. That meant someday I would leave Port Huron. She said Port Huron was her home and she was staying. As soon I was back in Port Huron, I went to her parents' house to tell her I was staying. But she wasn't home. Her mother said she would tell her to call me.

When I arrived at my room at Dorothy Myers' house, my phone was ringing. Calmly, I answered and sat down in the big chair.

"Hello, Mike," the now-familiar voice said. "This is Gil Stein in Maine. I've been thinking. I know what Harlan told you, but I saw how hard you hustled in covering the coach's press conference; I know the work you have done toward helping us learn about our area as we get started. What I'm thinking since you left is that I want a Bobby Clarke, not a Guy Lafleur."

He proceeded to explain the analogy.

"Bobby Clarke is a bundle of energy and wins championships on hard work," said Stein, a Philadelphia native. "Guy Lafleur has a lot of natural ability and flair, and he uses that to win games and championships. The Flyers are about hard work. And I want a Bobby Clarke.

So, I am overruling Harlan Singer and am offering you the job. It pays $10,000."

As excited as I was about the Maine opportunity, I was frustrated to be back where I was in 1973 when I was haggling with John Wismer for a livable wage.

Although I had started in Port Huron four years earlier at $8,300, I was now earning $13,500 thanks to doing two jobs and Morris Snider's generosity. I didn't want to take a step back financially no matter how desirable the job was.

"Mr. Stein, I am so thrilled that you called back," I said, "but I am making $13,500 right now and—despite the great opportunity—I cannot take that substantial a pay cut to move to a larger city."

Stein said, "Give me a minute."

In the years since, he has never said how much of our conversation he recalled. But I envisioned him going to giant ledger books, scanning down one column after another trying to determine where he could find some extra money. Perhaps he just went to the refrigerator and grabbed a can of soda.

He was off the phone for 30 seconds, but it seemed like 30 minutes.

"Okay," Stein said, "Eddie Snider's going to kill me, but I'll give you $14,000."

I immediately accepted. When I went back over to tell Joyce, she was there this time. We were both disappointed and excited at the same time. She wanted what was best for me. And, this had been forecasted for four years. It just always seemed so far in the distance. Mixed emotions all around. I had three weeks to finish up my first hockey job before driving all my belongings on to the second hockey job.

After a few weeks in Maine, I knew it had been a good decision to join this organization.

I found an apartment on a scenic little cove in Cape Elizabeth. Each morning, even when there was heavy fog, I could see the lobstermen guiding their boats into the cove to check their lobster traps. Considering I had grown up in the cornfields of Indiana, this was both fascinating and picturesque.

The only problem with the job was that Joyce was nearly 1,000 miles away. We talked frequently but it wasn't enough.

One Sunday in August, a month before training camp started, I placed "the call." I told her that it was obvious the team was going to be a success in Portland and my future looked brighter. I said I understood how much she loved living in her Michigan hometown. I asked whether she would at least come out and visit, to see if she might like the area and then become engaged.

"I'm sorry, but no," she said.

Coincidentally, I did hear from her twin brother and his wife shortly thereafter. They wanted to take a vacation before school started and said they were hoping to visit me. I offered them the use of my apartment. I'm sure they made a favorable report when they returned to Port Huron, but I had accepted that all bets were off. It seemed like my courtship of Joyce was over.

I buried myself in my job because there was plenty to do. The team had a staff of seven in the summer, and that included McCammon. We were all busy selling tickets and advertising. Stein had a clear business vision about how we were going to sell tickets. No discounts. He wanted fans to believe they were getting a product that was worth every cent they were paying.

One day McCammon seemed frustrated by a conversation he had with Stein.

"I don't understand Gil," McCammon said. "One business was going to buy 75 season tickets. They asked Gil to throw two more in for free. He wouldn't do it. Do you know how much money that is?"

Stein decided to explain his decision to the potential ticket-buyer this way: "We provide full value for the price of the ticket. We cannot be favoring one business over another, nor can we show our product is sub-standard by discounting it. That's how we are going to do it."

The local businessman did buy the 75 tickets at full value.

Stein knew what he was talking about because there was genuine excitement about the team in Portland.

When our first preseason schedule was finalized, you will never guess where the Mariners' first preseason game was going to be played: Port Huron, Michigan. I'm reasonably sure that McCammon's influence had something to do with that. It would have been easy for Bob to call Morris Snider and set up a game in McMorran Arena.

As soon as I heard, I reconnected with Joyce. I explained the surprise return and told her I would provide tickets for anyone she wanted to bring. She said she would bring two of her girlfriends. The Mariners beat the St. Louis Blues' B team, although NHLers Bob and Barclay Plager played that night.

Joyce and I only had time to talk briefly after the game, but we agreed to resume phone calls. Our relationship was not over.

WHAT WAS ESTABLISHED FROM THE beginning was that the Maine Mariners were not going to be a nickel-and-dime organization and they were going to be competitive. They were also the Flyers' farm team and that meant they were going to be tough. It was always uncomfortable to play against the Flyers' Broad Street Bullies and the same was going to be true of the Mariners. Half of the team was skilled, and the other half could fight. Early on, the Mariners boasted what we the called "The Four-H Club"; Dave Hoyda, Rene Hamelin, Al Hill, and Dave Hynek were all tough players.

When the team started 4–8–3, meetings were held. Keith Allen came down to watch the Mariners play and told McCammon, "We're going to get you some better players. We are not good enough right now."

Within 10 days, Allen brought in new backup goalie Grant Cole plus former-IHL 50-goal scorer Paul Evans, and he made a trade with the Minnesota North Stars to land scorer Blake Dunlop. He then reacquired defenseman Terry Murray from the Detroit Red Wings. Murray had played 153 NHL games before he suited up for the Mariners.

The day after Murray joined our team, New Haven Nighthawks public relations director Roy Mlakar called me and, noting our influx of talent, said: "I didn't know the Calder Cup [the AHL championship trophy] was for sale."

Mlakar would go on to become president of the Ottawa Senators and an executive with the Los Angeles Kings and Pittsburgh Penguins.

Those deals had the desired impact. We were much improved and quickly established that we were going to be one of the better AHL teams. Because of the Mariners' toughness, the team was intimidating.

In one memorable December game against the Hampton Gulls in the Cumberland County Civic Center, our penchant for roughness ran afoul of crusty, fiery Gulls coach John Brophy, who was no stranger to tough hockey. Brophy's team was the farm team for the World Hockey Association's Birmingham Bulls and the Gulls liked to play what was called "old-time hockey." The Mariners won the game easily, on a 5–0 Rick St. Croix shutout, but the game ended with Brophy spitting mad at the Mariners. In the closing seconds, our leading scorer Hill, playing physical hockey until the last whistle, lined up Gulls player Pat Donnelly and drove him into the Plexiglas behind the net. Donnelly suffered a broken nose.

Brophy was incensed. He said Hill would pay for that hit. "There's always a next time," Brophy said.

As fate would have it, the Mariners and Gulls were scheduled to play again in Maine the following month. It was a Saturday night and fans were eager to see whether the Gulls were indeed going to target Hill and push back hard against the Mariners. Brophy tipped his hand by persuading the Bulls to demote noted WHA tough guys Frank "Never" Beaton, Gilles "Bad News" Bilodeau, and Dave "Killer" Hanson for one game only.

The problem with Brophy's plan was that there were no direct flights from Birmingham, Alabama, to Portland, Maine. After playing a WHA game on a Friday night, the trio of tough guys flew to New York. But when they landed at LaGuardia, they were told the flight to Portland was canceled due to fog. With no chance to get to the game on time, the WHA tough guys returned to Birmingham. The Mariners took down the Gulls again.

Later that season, before the Gulls and Mariners met again, the Gulls folded. Thus, Al Hill never paid a price for breaking Donnelly's nose.

Every team in the league was having difficulty dealing with the Mariners' blend of toughness and skill. By Christmas, the Mariners led the AHL. Four days after Christmas, the Mariners shocked the hockey world by beating Moscow Dynamo 1–0. Even NHL teams had difficulty coping with the Russian skill in those days.

My first season in Maine was both memorable and fun-filled.

One of my favorite players on the Mariners' inaugural team was a tough guy named Brian Burke who would go on to become a Harvard-trained lawyer, a player agent, an NHL executive in charge of supplemental discipline, and finally a general manager for the Hartford

Whalers, Vancouver Canucks, Anaheim Ducks, Toronto Maple Leafs, and Calgary Flames. Today, he's an analyst for Rogers Television.

When I met Burke, he was a very entertaining young player with a high level of intelligence and overflowing wit and charm. He was a fan favorite, although that could have been said about everyone on the team.

But Burkie was always fun. When the Mariners' wives put together a cookbook, Burke insisted on submitting his favorite breakfast. It was called Oreos and Milk. Here is the recipe he submitted: "Crush up a handful of Oreos into large glass. Add milk. Eat."

Easy-to-follow directions.

After the Mariners' first season, Burke decided to go back to school to become a lawyer. While studying at Harvard, he drove down to the Big E Coliseum in Springfield, Massachusetts, to see his former Mariners teammates playing against the Springfield Indians.

Knowing the Maine fans would love to hear from Burke, I invited him to be my color analyst. He was happy to do it. He put on a headset and mic and provided the colorful ad libs you would expect from him.

It was going fine until the second period when there was a ruckus behind the Maine bench. Some of the Mariners and some of the fans started to exchange words. Then sticks were raised. Shoving between players and fans occurred. That's when I lost my color analyst.

"Sorry, Doc," he said on air. "But I got to go down and help the boys."

I was treated to seeing some of Burke's strengths on display that night, particularly his roundhouse rights.

Life with the Mariners was never without adventure and laughter. One year, the Mariners had to endure a 14-hour bus trip from Maine to Halifax, Nova Scotia, Canada. You saw the Maine countryside and then into New Brunswick and then around the Bay of Fundy before pulling into Halifax. The Nova Scotia Voyageurs, the Montreal Canadiens' top farm team, and the Mariners became instant rivals because the Voyageurs won the Calder Cup in 1976 and 1977 and the Mariners won in 1978 and 1979.

Stein always believed the "quickest way to love the Mariners is to know one personally." Our mission was to introduce our team to the public as often in possible. Because the Flyers always wanted to be known as a first-class organization, our players always wore coats and ties when they were in public. We explored Maine's hinterlands. I recall traveling 90 miles with players Yves Preston and M.F. Schurman to introduce them to a group of 50 people.

Once, we visited the Cape Elizabeth Lions Club. One elderly gentleman came up to me afterward and said: "They seem like nice boys, but we really don't cahten to raisen' baby Flyahs up he-yuh."

I guess he was a Bruins fan.

Another time I accompanied scrappy defenseman Frank Bathe to a school visit, and a spunky eighth-grader asked what it felt like sitting in a penalty box.

"Well," Bathe said quickly, "it's like being in school."

Players say the darndest things.

Minor league teams love their promotions, and the Mariners used the traditional hockey Score-O game as the main promotion. Two lucky fans were chosen through a lucky number in the game program, and each of them was eligible to play Score-O between the first and second period before the ice was resurfaced by the Zamboni.

Each contestant was stationed at the blue line and given a puck to shoot toward the net, which was covered by a wooden cutout with a six-inch hole cut out at the bottom. If the lucky shooter shot the puck 60 feet into the hole, their prize was a 21-inch portable color television. That was a significant prize in those days.

That was the first round. Then, the shooters were turned around and asked to fire a puck toward the other net. That's a 120-foot shot. Plus, the opening has been reduced to four inches. That's a tight fit for a puck that is one inch high and three inches in diameter.

There's good reason for the 120-foot shot to be challenging: the prize was a new Chevy Chevette.

If no one won the car during the season, the plan was to give it away in a drawing at the final home game. Two contestants were identified, and they came out and shot for the television and car.

They missed on the car shot and everyone in the arena cheered because that meant everyone in the arena had a chance at winning the automobile.

Our radio feed went statewide, and Frank Fixaris, sports director for WGAN-TV, the CBS affiliate, filled the intermission with interviews and scoring summaries. But with an automobile giveaway on tap, Frank and I stayed with a live feed to talk about who won.

The car was driven onto the ice. The New England Chevy dealers were all introduced. Mariners captain Dennis Patterson came out of the dressing room to draw the winning ticket. Mariners marketing director Frank Gilbert was the emcee for the drawing ceremony. With memorable fanfare, the winning ticket was drawn, and Gilbert gleefully announced, "The winner of the Chevrolet Chevette is…Sue Hamilton!"

About 10 rows below our broadcast perch, a young woman let out a joyously loud scream. She was jumping up and down and waving toward the ice below. She was the winner and wanted to make sure everyone knew it.

She was escorted down the stairs by the usher and was greeted with enthusiastic applause as she stepped onto the red carpet laid on the ice. Even though she was wearing stylish heels, she hurried across the ice at a good pace.

After she arrived at the car, the Chevrolet representative shook her hand and handed her the keys. It was a wonderful moment. There was only one problem.

Gilbert looked down the ice and noticed that an usher was trying to get his attention. He was motioning wildly and pointing to a woman standing next to him.

Now, what do you think the odds were that there would be two women named Sue Hamilton attending that game?

It was a longshot to be sure, but it happened that night.

Under his breath, Patterson chuckled and uttered a two-word profanity that any player would have said in that situation because he immediately recognized the second Sue Hamilton as a woman who was dating one of the players.

As the second Sue Hamilton was hustled onto the ice, a chant started to wind around the Civic Center: "Two cars. Two cars. Two cars…"

The Chevrolet representative whispered to Gilbert during the chaos. "Get me out of here," he said. "I cannot give away two cars."

With both Sue Hamiltons standing side-by-side, and thousands more listening on the Mariners' radio network, the tickets were compared. The second Sue Hamilton had the winning number.

The "Two cars" chant grew louder as the keys were taken away from Sue Hamilton No. 1. With that, there was a hasty exit from the ice. Sue Hamilton No. 1 was escorted to Ed Anderson's office.

Thanks to some deft work by Anderson, Sue Hamilton No. 1 didn't fare badly. In addition to receiving numerous apologies, she received the color television, season tickets for the following season, and free dinners at every restaurant listed in our program.

In my first AHL season, the Mariners rolled down the homestretch, winning the division and earning a bye in the first round. Evans and Dunlop, acquired by Allen after the poor start, were two of our top five leading scorers. Dunlop (82 points in 62 games) won the Les Cunningham Award as the AHL's most valuable player. Murray, another player acquired by Allen, won the Eddie Shore Award as the league's best defenseman. McCammon won the Louis A.R. Pieri Award as coach of the year.

The Mariners needed seven physical games to defeat the Nova Scotia Voyageurs in the semifinals to set up a final matchup against the Nighthawks. Slow-talking farm boy goalie Pete Peeters, called up mid-winter, was on an impressive roll in the postseason. He was living out of the Portlander Hotel. He bought the *Portland Press Herald* newspaper every day, but then placed them on a stack.

"I'll read them in the summer," he said.

Peeters outdueled New Haven goalie Doug Soetaert and the Mariners won the series in five games. Fans came over the glass to take part in the on-ice celebration and the parade of the Calder Cup that wound around the ice.

The Mariners were given a parade in Portland. The mayor held a ceremony at city hall. Our bumper stickers changed from "Maine Mariners" to a picture of the Calder Cup with the words "Maine Loves the Mariners."

For a young broadcaster, it was the season you dreamed of having.

THE PHILADELPHIA
STORY

When the Philadelphia Flyers offered me my first job doing television play-by-play for NHL games in 1979, I politely declined.

You are reading that correctly. I turned down a chance to be in The Show.

At the time, I was 33 and my life already seemed too good to be true.

Midway through my first season in Portland, Joyce had a change of heart and decided to visit to see if she could live there. She and two of her girlfriends drove 759 miles from Port Huron.

Joyce liked the city and said she was open to moving there to be with me. That's all I needed to hear. I didn't want to take a chance that she would change her mind.

I invited her back out for Easter. After the Mariners defeated the Hershey Bears on Easter Sunday, we all retreated to Bob and Marie McCammon's home. Port Huron newspaperman Ted Findlay was also visiting as McCammon's guest.

I handed Joyce an envelope, and she removed a card adorned with a traditional bunny and Easter egg on the front. When she opened the card, a check slipped out. It was endorsed for the exact amount of a wedding ring that she had been eyeing at Kay's Jewelers in a nearby mall.

"Go buy it," I wrote on the card.

Probably my proposal doesn't seem romantic to you, but it was meaningful to both of us because I was asking her to marry me in the home of the McCammons, who were the first to suggest we might be a good match.

We were married on July 1 at the Port Huron church that had sponsored the first "singles night" where we met. The reception was held at the formal lower lounge of Port Huron's McMorran Arena. Morris waived the fee for me. We honeymooned in Paris and London, and the Mariners, at the behest of Ed Anderson, paid for that trip as a wedding gift.

The Vivians sat in the first row during the ceremony. Jack was at the front of the reception line. As I walked up to shake his hand, he said, laughing, "Win a championship and you get careless." Joyce laughed too.

I didn't feel careless. I felt overjoyed. By the summer of 1979, I had been married for only a year when Flyers president Bob Butera and director of broadcasting Pete Silverman offered me a contract to broadcast 35 games for PRISM cable. I would also share the in-truck producer role with Silverman for the road games. The timing of the job wasn't good. Joyce and I were buying our first house in south Portland.

But that wasn't the only reason I declined. I already had a job I enjoyed very much. The Mariners had won two Calder Cup championships in their first two seasons of existence. They were favored to make it three in a row.

McCammon was still behind the Portland bench. He had started the 1978–79 season as the Flyers coach, while Pat Quinn was the Portland coach. But McCammon only lasted 50 games before the Flyers demoted him to Portland and brought Quinn to coach the Flyers.

It was an impossible ask for McCammon to follow Fred Shero, who had taken the Flyers to back-to-back Stanley Cup championships. Plus, Quinn had been Shero's assistant coach, and players wanted him as Shero's successor. It was a can't-win situation for McCammon from the beginning.

Coincidentally, the Mariners were scheduled to play in Philadelphia as part of an AHL-NHL doubleheader. The Mariners were going to play the Philadelphia Firebirds in the afternoon game at the Spectrum, and the Flyers were scheduled to take on the Atlanta Flames that night. The coaching changes were announced before the doubleheader.

Maine's captain Dennis Patterson was the interim coach that afternoon because our team president Ed Anderson couldn't initially persuade McCammon to accept the Mariners job. But McCammon did eventually come back and was behind the bench for the Mariners' second consecutive championship.

It was an odd situation, right down to the fact that the McCammons took over the house that the Quinns were renting on the ocean in Portland.

I liked Pat. A broadcaster and coach spend a lot of time together on the road because the coach doesn't hang out with players. I learned from him about the game and about life.

He used to say that too many players "spend what they earn" instead of embracing a long-term plan. I vowed if I ever made the NHL as a broadcaster, I would follow Pat's advice and save all that I could.

What I didn't miss when Pat left were his cigars. He smoked them continuously, and players started embracing the habit. The smoke and the smell on an enclosed three-hour bus ride to Springfield were sometimes unbearable.

But I have fond memories of going out after a game with Pat and his wife, Sandra, to an Irish bar in Portland.

Even now, I can picture him pounding on our table, tapping out the beat and singing along to "What Shall We Do with a Drunken Sailor." Pat enjoyed life, and I enjoyed him. He died in 2014.

As much as I enjoyed Pat, I was looking forward to working with McCammon again in Portland.

Also, right or wrong, doing play-by-play on pay cable for 35 games didn't seem to me to be a better job than broadcasting every game for the Maine Mariners. That's just how I felt.

I didn't believe this would be the only chance I would ever receive to broadcast in the NHL. Before I was offered the Flyers job, I was told that Hartford Whalers owner Howard Baldwin, a former Flyers ticket manager, had called Flyers owner Ed Snider and asked for permission to talk to me about becoming the Whalers' radio voice.

Snider refused to grant permission. Instead, the Whalers hired Chuck Kaiton, who ended up being a Hall of Fame broadcaster and president of the NHL Broadcasters Association. They made the right choice.

I was thankful the Flyers didn't seem annoyed by my decision to stay in Portland. Silverman ended up doing the play-by-play at home and was the producer on the road.

The Mariners' season didn't end up being as lengthy as I expected it to be. They were eliminated in the semifinals by the New Brunswick Hawks, who were led by three highly skilled players who would go on to become notable NHL coaches. Bruce Boudreau (36 goals and 90 points in 75 games) was the Hawks' leading scorer. Darryl Sutter was second with 35 goals. Ron Wilson, with 20 goals in 43 games, was a dominant puck-moving defenseman.

Meanwhile, the Flyers, now coached by Pat Quinn, reached the Stanley Cup Final, where they were playing the New York Islanders.

The reason I know the Flyers didn't harbor a grudge over me rejecting their job offer was that Butera invited Joyce and me to be his guests at a Stanley Cup Final game in Philadelphia. My hunch was that they wanted us to see that life in the NHL with a big-market team could be exciting.

Keep in mind that Joyce had lived in Port Huron with a population under 30,000, and none of my stops could be described as a bustling metropolis. My list included LaFontaine, Oxford (Ohio), Beaver Falls (Pennsylvania), Bowling Green (Ohio), Port Huron, and Portland. The population of Portland is about 67,000, and that made it the largest city I ever lived in.

By contrast, Philadelphia, the sixth-largest American city, has 1.5 million people living within its borders. The number swells to 6 million when you count the greater Philadelphia area.

The Spectrum was rocking the night of our visit. The atmosphere was nuclear. It was exciting to see Bill Barber, Bobby Clarke, and Reggie Leach roaring up the ice. Brian Propp. Ken Linseman. Paul Holmgren. The Flyers had a collection of memorable players. The team also had a handful of ex-Mariners, including goalie Pete Peeters, who had helped the Mariners win their first Calder Cup. Rick St. Croix was the No. 3 goalie. Dennis Patterson was on the roster. It was an exciting night.

After the game, Joyce and I were ushered into the director's lounge for an audience with Ed Snider and his wife, Myrna. It wasn't a social call. It was about another job offer. While there was no strong-arming, they said they appreciated my abilities and wanted to see them in Philadelphia.

By then, Stein was working for the NHL and Anderson had assumed the role of Mariners president. He agreed with the Flyers that it was time for me to take the next step.

"I think you've gotten about as good at writing press releases as a man is going to get," Anderson said. "The Flyers want you to take your career further and help them. We would be thrilled to have you stay… but they have already asked you once."

Joyce and I talked it over and it was decided I wasn't going to decline their offer a second time. Six months after becoming first-time home-owners, we planted a "For Sale" sign on our front lawn in South Portland.

BEING HIRED BY THE FLYERS was much different than my hiring experience in Portland and Port Huron. Instead of fretting over nickels and dimes, I found myself being treated like an important hire. We were met at the airport by noted real estate guru Ed Parvin. The Flyers assigned him to help us find a house. We toured 25 homes over three visits to Philadelphia.

We pulled into the driveway of house No. 26, and Parvin pulled out a fresh-on-the-market mobile phone to see if we were welcome. While we marveled at the technological advances we were witnessing, Parvin received the go-ahead to enter the premises.

As soon as Joyce walked in, she said: "This is the one."

"Don't you want to look around the house?" Parvin asked.

"Of course," Joyce said. "But I'm telling you right now, this is the one."

She was right. We waited in the car while Parvin submitted our offer to the agency offering the listing.

When he returned to the car, he said: "I'm sorry but I had to increase your offer by $1,000 because someone else made an offer higher than your first offer. You should get the house now."

We did. In that era, interest rates were around 16 percent. But Parvin found us a mortgage for 14.5 percent. Can you imagine being thrilled by a 14.5 percent interest rate? We were. Maybe the transition would have been smooth without Parvin, but the Flyers' first-class treatment made the move much easier for Joyce and me. I wanted my wife to be happy and she was.

I know I was happy, because 20 years after I had discovered the joy of hockey at the Coliseum in Fort Wayne, I was going to be an NHL broadcaster.

My first NHL broadcast of any kind was a preseason game, at the Spectrum, between the Flyers and Canadiens in September 1980.

Because we hadn't yet completed our move to Philadelphia, I flew down just to do the broadcast. Former Flyers players Bobby Taylor and Ed Van Impe were my color commentators.

What I remember most about that day was how easy it was to identify the players. We were stationed in the lower press box, which was at center ice, in the lower level stands. Sometimes the play would be 30 feet in front of us.

Plus, the Canadiens had already made their final cuts, meaning varsity players were in this game, not minor-leaguers whose names I may or may not have known before reviewing the roster. In 1980, only a few Canadiens were wearing helmets and no Philadelphia player was wearing one.

It was easy picking out big Larry Robinson or Guy Lafleur, Guy Lapointe, or Serge Savard, when they took the ice. Likewise, I had no trouble identifying Clarke, Barber, or Leach.

Other than suffering a bout of nervousness, I felt reasonably confident calling the game. Plus, Bobby and Ed liked to have a good time so they made sure to rib me about said nervousness. It was their way of welcoming me aboard, and who knows, maybe it made me more comfortable.

After the game, producer Pete Silverman's assistant, Mike Finocchiaro, later an award-winning producer himself, took me on a guided tour of the city, including a stop at Pat's Cheese Steaks.

The other fact I remember from that night was that I walked back to the Hilton Hotel, located two blocks from the Spectrum, after the game. The next morning, I heard that there had been a mob hit in the Hilton's parking lot the night before.

I realized then that I wasn't in Portland anymore.

PRISM was a pay cable outlet, meaning it was a smaller audience than Taylor and Van Impe had when they were on over-the-air TV with

Gene Hart. I thought they seemed more relaxed with their comments on our broadcasts.

It was a good gig for them. We only did home games, and the Flyers won most of those games. There was no criticism that needed to be done. This was the early 1980s, meaning fighting still played a major role. Both Taylor and Van Impe were proponents of a rough brand of hockey.

"You've got a whole career to pay a guy back," Van Impe was fond of saying.

When asked about the heavy hit he laid on Valeri Kharlamov at the Spectrum, which caused the Soviet Red Army team to leave on January 11, 1976, Van Impe would say: "It wasn't a penalty and it got me on *The Mike Douglas Show.*" It was broadcast from Philadelphia at the time.

Taylor had been a backup goalie, and that meant he rarely played, and when he did, it was on the road against strong offensive teams like the Boston Bruins or the Bobby Hull–led Chicago Blackhawks. That background gave him good material for some of the comedy he would try on our broadcasts.

"Bobby Hull'd come down the first time on the left wing and he'd crank one right at your head," Taylor would say. "Then the second time, it'd be right at your feet. The first one would whistle off the glass. The second one would go in."

I was so new to the NHL that I felt I could benefit from some good practices before the season began.

That's why in late September 1980, I had made a road trip on the Jersey Turnpike to New York's Madison Square Garden with our Gene Hart–led television crew for a preseason game with the Rangers. I was in a car with Hart, the legendary voice of the Flyers, along with Silverman, the producer, and Taylor, who would provide the color. Officially, I was going to observe the game as a Flyers employee for the first time. Carrying a battery-powered recorder, my plan was to broadcast the game to myself as a tune-up for what was to come.

This was the night I learned that nothing is quite that simple in the broadcasting world, and that unions held considerable power in major cities.

Making conversation on the ride, I asked Hart what Madison Square Garden was like.

"You are going to hate it, Doc," Hart said. "You are so far away. You are low. And the Rangers' [white] home jerseys are so faint under the lights that you have a hard time making out the numbers. You just have to learn the line combinations and take a chance on the far winger. You don't have a chance."

Then he paused, before adding: "But the food in the press box is the best in the league."

Shortly after our arrival, Silverman whispered to me that I "may not be able to broadcast my game into my recorder."

The union was balking. "The shop steward said they would have to call a man in to hit the play-record button" on my machine, Silverman reported.

My "machine" was a hand-held recorder. The union position seemed preposterous.

Right after I consumed the much-heralded press meal—and Hart was right about its quality—Silverman informed me that the union had signed off on me doing my own button-pushing. But it was a good lesson for me about how business was done at the NHL level.

A few years later, when I was broadcasting a Devils game, I was in a meeting at Madison Square Garden when a member of the hierarchy said he wanted to start with a riddle.

"How many Garden electricians does it take to change a light bulb?" he asked.

When no one answered, he said: "Twenty-six. Do you have a problem with that?"

We chuckled at the joke, but we all understood that unions have power that must be respected when you are a broadcaster.

There is a real answer for that question, one I discovered when I was preparing for a Capitals vs. Rangers playoff game at the Garden several years later. It was 5:00 PM, two hours before the puck drop. The arena was empty. I was in a distant broadcast booth in semi-darkness trying to write some notes on my scorecard. The light bulb directly above me was burned out. J.T. Townsend, our floor director, asked the electrician if we could get the bulb changed. Immediately, the man pushed a ladder over, scrambled up the rungs, and switched the bulb.

I was standing at the foot of his ladder, preparing to express my appreciation and thankfulness for his effort, when he said: "It's usually three of us for this."

We will take that as the real answer for the riddle.

It wasn't only in New York. The Forum in Inglewood, California, where the Los Angeles Kings used to play, had a strong union presence.

When I was working as a producer, I wanted Taylor to go down the hallway and interview a player after a game and then go back to Hart for the final word. Seeing how it was 1:00 AM in Philadelphia, it wasn't a big deal one way or the other. But I thought it would be better if we could get both men on camera. That would mean a light would have to be turned on in both locations. But only one electrician had been assigned to work with us. Through the powers of persuasion, we convinced the union steward to allow the lone electrician to turn on Hart's light and then go downstairs to turn on Taylor's light. No extra charge.

Later, I learned that a Los Angeles shop steward had once agreed to a similar request only if he was given an authentic Flyers jersey that had been previously set aside in case Philadelphia needed an emergency goalie.

The NHL was a much different world than the minor leagues. The first time the Flyers passed out meal money for a road trip I received an envelope with $350 cash. It was the most cash I had ever seen at one time.

Hart turned out to be prophetic when he said I wasn't going to like the Rangers' broadcast location because it was a good distance from the ice. Calling the game from farther away turned out to be the biggest adjustment I had to make as an NHL broadcaster.

Minor league arenas are generally small and quaint structures, with broadcast locations that are relatively close to the ice.

Chicago Stadium was still in business when I started broadcasting in the NHL and it had a broadcast location that rivaled any I had in the minors.

In that historic venue, booths were in a bucket suspended from the first balcony. You were only about 15 rows back. It was a wonderful location, but most NHL booths were higher and farther away than I was in the minors.

Moving to the NHL was also a lifestyle change. In the minors, you bus to a game, get there a couple of hours before, and then head back home. You rarely stay in a hotel. As an NHL team broadcaster, you leave home for three or four days, or a week, or sometimes longer. We spent many nights in quality hotels.

In my early years, I spent plenty of time with Gene Hart because neither one of us were into heavy drinking and nightlife. Hart liked opera and museums on off nights and occasionally I would join him.

What I liked to do on off nights was go to a sporting event. I remember the Flyers were on a road trip and due to play in Winnipeg on January 2. Hart and I purposely flew in early to see Winnipeg play the Washington Capitals on New Year's Eve. It seemed like we were in the Arctic when we arrived in the city. It was bitterly cold. That was the first time I saw cars plugged into outlets on the streets to assure that they would start the next morning.

The Capitals were staying in the same hotel we were in and Gene and I rang in the new year with them because we didn't have anywhere else to go. As soon the clock struck midnight, I went up to my room, called Joyce, and went to bed.

When I look back at that time, it feels like it was too much lost time on the road. We didn't have anything to do on New Year's Day so I just watched football in my room. But it seemed very exciting to me at the time, because I had just arrived in the NHL. Joyce was very understanding.

THE FLYERS TREATED ME WELL. But in 1983, Butera, who had moved to the New Jersey Devils, offered me a full-time television job. Plus, Silverman had moved to Madison Square Garden and that network had the Devils' rights. It was a good fit for me.

Joyce and I didn't even bother to move. We stayed in Cherry Hill, and I made a longer commute when I had to work in New York. By then, Joyce was working in the Flyers' ticket office and her bosses wanted her to stay.

The other change my promotion to the NHL brought about was the hiring of an agent.

I didn't need one as a minor league broadcaster. John Wismer or Gil Stein would have laughed at me had I suggested that he needed to negotiate with my agent.

Right after I signed on to work at MSG, I received a call from agent Art Kaminsky's office. I was informed that Kaminsky wanted to represent me.

Kaminsky had garnered plenty of attention in the early 1980s through his representation of coach Herb Brooks and many of the members of the 1980 U.S. Olympic team.

When I received that call, I didn't know much about agents other than most bosses didn't like to deal with them.

After mentioning that to the caller, I was told that Kaminsky understood all of that, but knew how to develop a relationship that was good for everyone.

That may be the case, I said, but I only just agreed to terms with MSG and there was not much Kaminsky's firm could do for me.

But Kaminsky didn't give up. MSG sent me to the 1984 draft to file reports on the Devils' draft picks. While I was there, Kaminsky invited me to his suite for a chat.

He said he would represent me, without fee, until it was time for my next contract negotiation. Of course, he would negotiate that deal for his usual fee. In the meantime, he would look for additional work for me for a 10 percent fee. I liked Art and it seemed like a reasonable offer.

The agreement with him paid off because he worked with Stein to persuade ESPN to give me a shot as a national broadcaster in 1986.

I needed that work because my Devils work was disappearing, not by my choice.

In 1986, Madison Square Garden decided not to go after the Devils' rights. SportsChannel America, as the only bidder, dictated terms. The new network wanted me to stay on the Devils broadcasts but wanted to pay me 40 percent less than I had been earning. Despite a noble effort, Butera could not persuade SportsChannel to improve its offer.

Unwilling to take such a large cut, I found myself out of work. That's when Kaminsky earned his fee.

Given the history of the Rangers-Flyers rivalry, what happened next is quite remarkable. The two teams cooperated in helping me carve the equivalent of full-time employment.

MSG executive Bob Gutkowski hired me as a backup to Marv Albert on Rangers radio broadcasts and Flyers president Jay Snider hired me as a part-time host on Flyers telecasts on Philly 57.

MSG sold advertising based on Albert's presence, but I ended up doing more than half of the games. At the time, Albert was doing football, baseball, and boxing, plus other assignments.

Kaminsky worked out the details, and it ended up working extremely well. It certainly helped that I am not a person who causes anger when I leave. I had thanked everyone in the Flyers organization before taking the Devils job.

Presumably, it also helped that Joyce continued to be a Flyers employee. Joyce worked during normal business hours at the Spectrum as well as during games. Fans sometimes referred to her as "the Canadian girl" because the Michigan accent can sometimes sound a bit like the Canadian accent. The confusion is more understandable when you know that Joyce was born two miles from the Canadian border.

In 1988, ESPN broadcaster Ken Wilson had conflicts in his schedule and I was brought in to work with analyst Bill Clement, who had played for the Flyers on their back-to-back Stanley Cup champions in 1974 and 1975. Suddenly, I was a national broadcaster.

I had instant chemistry with Clement. We were a good team. He had a comedic flair. I can play the straight man. We were like Laurel and Hardy.

As it turned out, it was important that I didn't burn any bridges in Philadelphia and it was important that Clement had a Flyers connection.

6
THE BEGINNING
AND THE END

Philadelphia Flyers executive Jay Snider, son of owner Ed Snider, met with me at the 1988 All-Star Game in St. Louis and dropped a bomb.

He wanted me to replace legendary Gene Hart as the Flyers' television play-by-play man and have Gene move to the radio.

Hart was as popular as most Philadelphia players. This wasn't going to be well received by the fan base. Snider knew it and I knew it.

Hart had been the team's TV voice since shortly after the Flyers joined the NHL in the 1967–68 expansion. He was a beloved figure in the community. After all, he had been in the booth when the Broad Street Bullies had dominated the NHL. He was 57 at the time, much younger than I am today as an NBC broadcaster. The Flyers were keeping Hart on the radio broadcast with his analyst and ex-Flyers goalie Bobby Taylor.

But that wasn't going to be enough to appease the fan base.

Job offers are supposed to be exciting. This one was not. It was stressful, especially since Gene had no idea what was happening.

As much as I wanted to be a full-time NHL play-by-play guy, I didn't want it coming at the expense of Gene losing his job. I viewed Gene as a mentor. We lived only a few blocks from each other, and sometimes rode to the game together. We were friends and colleagues. The first week I was in Philadelphia, Gene and his wife, Sarah, invited Joyce and me to their home to meet their children. My wish would have been to catch on with another NHL team, not replace Gene Hart.

Snider must have sensed my discomfort, because he added this line to our conversation.

"This will happen, whether you accept the job or not," Snider said. "If you don't take it, we will offer it to someone else."

Snider said former Flyers player Bill Clement was being offered the job as color analyst. That would give me plenty of familiarity and continue the Stanley Cup link with the fan base that Bobby Taylor also had.

I felt bad for Gene, but there was nothing I could have done to get him back on television. The Snider family had decided Gene's health was an issue. They decided they wanted to make a move before it got worse.

Even though I was in an awkward position, I decided to take the job. Clement and I both agreed to five-year contracts. We were paid well. That was certainly the most security I had ever had in this business.

I knew full well that following Gene was an impossible task. I didn't blame Philadelphia fans for being unhappy with the decision. At least Bill had a following because he had played on the back-to-back Stanley Cup champions. But I had just done pay cable and been a background person. I couldn't be Gene Hart. I never tried to be.

The Flyers knew that this was going to be a bumpy ride, but they really didn't know how to make it easier.

You always want everyone to like you, but you know that's never going to be the case. Even today, you are going to find people who don't like my broadcasting style. That's just part of the business.

Philadelphia fans are not shy about voicing their opinions about what happens with their teams. The radio station WIP, the radio rights holder, urged fans to turn down the sound on the television and listen to Gene's call on the radio.

It was a challenging first season, but I never dwelled on it. Clement and I just learned to sidestep the brickbats thrown our way. Gene and I were neighbors and still occasionally rode to the games together. He understood the situation.

I DON'T KNOW IF FANS warmed up to me in the second season, but a health scare really brought some perspective to my life and career.

On Friday, October 19, 1990, while I was sitting in my hotel room in Montreal, a doctor said a word over the phone that made me instantly realize that my job approval rating didn't matter.

Cancer.

A biopsy taken earlier in the week in Hershey, Pennsylvania, showed that I had prostate cancer. The news was so stunning that I had no idea how to react.

As I hung up the phone, I at least had the presence of mind to say: "Dear God, help me get through this."

I didn't see it coming, although my doctor had tried to prepare me. My general practitioner, Warren Wolfe, felt something he called "suspicious" during a digital exam. But two ultrasounds came up normal. Given that I have some cancer in my family history, he wanted another test.

"Why don't you go to a different lab?" he said. "Just to be sure."

Because we were moving from Cherry Hill to Hershey, I decided to have the ultrasound in Hershey.

That ultrasound was also negative. The Hershey technician looked at my chart, and said: "You came all the way, 100 miles, from Cherry Hill for this ultrasound?"

I explained I was moving to Hershey soon.

"Well, since you've come this far, why don't you have a biopsy too," he said. "It doesn't hurt and then you will know for sure. Ultrasounds don't tell you everything."

The biopsy showed I had cancer.

Alone in my room with a game to broadcast the next day, I struggled to decide what to do. A friend, Bruce Cooper, who not only covered hockey but wrote extensive medical articles, gave me sound advice.

"Number one, I can't believe this type of cancer has metastasized, but you will find out when you get back," Cooper said. "And number two, you will want to tell Joyce in person. Don't call her. You have to sit with her face-to-face."

I decided to go to Bill Clement's room and tell him. "You have to call Jay Snider," Clement said.

The reason why Clement wanted me to call Snider is that he knew Snider would get the Flyers' medical staff involved. Professional sports teams usually have top-notch medical personnel.

Snider got me a Monday appointment with Isadore Brodsky, a prominent Philadelphia hematologist and oncologist who had worked with the Flyers wives' Fight for Life Carnival. Brodsky was the first doctor to do a stem-cell transplant in the Philadelphia area.

Before that appointment, I had to call a Saturday night game in Montreal. I don't remember how I got through it. I don't remember anything about the game. I didn't even remember the score until looking it up. (It was a 5–3 Flyers win for their sixth consecutive triumph.)

Realizing the angst that I was feeling, my producer Bryan Cooper said after the game: "Congratulations, that was a real achievement."

When I arrived back in New Jersey on Sunday, I sat with Joyce on the couch and told her about the diagnosis. "I don't know what the future will bring, but I know I will need your strength," I said.

She delivered that strength.

Prostate cancer didn't have the visibility in 1991 that it has today. Men didn't know as much about it as we know today. Since it had been caught early, Brodsky was optimistic about my prognosis. But he wanted me to go visit a specialist, Dr. Charles Brendler, at Johns Hopkins Hospital in Baltimore. He recommended a radical prostatectomy.

Back then, robotic surgery hadn't been perfected yet. He was performing old-school surgery and we talked about when we would do it.

"How about tomorrow?" I said.

He smiled. I liked his personality. It was reassuring. "I know you have cancer in your body and you want it out," he said. "But this cancer moves very slowly, and it is not something that is urgent. How about we wait until January, right after the holidays?"

Even though this seemed rather urgent to me, I put my trust in his expertise. He told me there was nothing to worry about and I chose to believe him.

As he was leaving, he jokingly said: "Oh, by the way, I just want you to know that I am a New York Rangers fan. But I'm going to give you the best care anyway."

I told him he would never have to pay for another hockey ticket ever again.

When he came into my room before the surgery, he noted that my window faced a brick wall. "That's because you are a Flyers announcer," he said, laughing.

He reassured me all along the way, and he was right in his diagnosis. It was early stage and an easily removable tumor. No chemotherapy. No radiation. I've been cancer-free for 29 years.

I asked Brendler what he could have done for me had my cancer diagnosis come 10 years earlier. "Not as much," he said.

My hospital stay was 16 days. It would be one day if I had that surgery today.

When I discuss my cancer scare, I like to remind everyone that "every day is a blessing." I also trumpet the need for people to have routine health tests.

Chaz Brendler is based in Chicago now, and I have made sure he has seen some games for free. He has never asked. I've sought him to see if he wanted to go watch his beloved Rangers.

The Flyers kept the situation quiet until the day after the surgery, when they announced that I was recovering well. The Snider family's concern about me was humbling. They looked after me in my time of need.

RESTORED TO HEALTH, I JUMPED excitedly back into my career. Even though I was a full-time Flyers broadcaster, I managed to broadcast some football games for CBS in 1992 and 1993. I mostly did games in September, before the NHL season started. I would temporarily replace Tim Ryan, who also had U.S. Open tennis responsibility.

CBS had the NFC rights in those days, and some weeks the network had six games, instead of five. In those weeks, I also worked if my Flyers duties didn't conflict.

Hank Stram was near the end of his career as an analyst, and he and I would work together when the sixth broadcast team was needed. He was a delightfully colorful character. When he traveled for games, he carried a four-foot cardboard garment box. He had two five-pound weights in the bottom of it because he liked to work out in his hotel room. He always gate-checked his garment box. He could do that back then because security wasn't what it is today. Plus, he was Hank Stram, former coach of the Super Bowl–winning Kansas City Chiefs. Sure, Hank, we will take care of you.

Stram was a good analyst, even though he mostly worked off the monitor. He did have a platform that he stood on if he wanted to look onto the field. Even back then, the camera coverage of the game was good enough to analyze by monitor. More than one analyst did it that way.

When I started doing the NFL, I tried to learn every player's number during the week. That was 53 guys on every team, a total of 106 guys.

Joyce would quiz me. When Tampa Bay was in my game, she would say "Orange 55" and I'd tell her who it was. Or "Green 26."

In hindsight, my whole process was counterproductive. Longtime broadcaster Verne Lundquist told me later, "Just learn the guys who will get the ball and a few key defensive guys. That's all you need."

One of my favorite Stram stories involves working with him on a Tampa Bay vs. Green Bay game at Lambeau Field on the last Sunday of November.

I was taller than Stram, but he would always start our conversations with, "Mike, you little rat."

So it was on the Monday before the game. "Mike, you little rat...you got to call CBS and get us a couple of those CBS parkas," Stram said over the phone. "They are worth about $200 and they have the CBS football logos."

Stram said it was going to be too cold to wear overcoats. I knew all of the stories about Lambeau's Frozen Tundra. I wasn't going to argue.

"We are going to be freezing," Stram said.

We both called CBS and were both assured that parkas would be waiting for us when we arrived on Friday. But when he landed in Green Bay, the parkas were nowhere to be seen.

Stram made his point and someone told him they would overnight the parkas to be there Saturday. Can you imagine how much it cost for overnight delivery 26 years ago? It was expensive, that's all I know for sure. But the parkas showed up Saturday.

When we got up Sunday morning in Green Bay, it was...55 and sunny. The parkas never came out of the bag. Stram took his home and I took mine with me. I still have it somewhere.

BACK AT THE FLYERS, PEOPLE were one thing and business was another for Ed Snider.

Going back to the first season I replaced Hart, Snider had taken issue with our style. He was disappointed that our broadcasts didn't reflect a pronounced rooting interest in the Flyers the way Hart's broadcasts had.

The primary reason was SportsChannel America had become the NHL's broadcast partner and it was simulcasting games to local markets. In other words, I would call a Philadelphia game for a national audience, meaning I needed to talk as much about the Flyers' opponent as I did about the Flyers. Meanwhile, that feed was going to Philadelphia and Mr. Snider sat in his home stewing and wondering why he was paying me to talk about Mario Lemieux or Rod Langway or whomever the opposing team's top player happened to be. I wasn't overly critical of the Flyers, but I was trying to maintain impartiality for the national broadcast.

What irked Mr. Snider even more was that SportsChannel was paying me for the same game he was paying me to broadcast.

I was sympathetic to Mr. Snider's position. It was his team. You want your owner to be passionate about his team. And Mr. Snider was.

He was particularly annoyed during the 1989 playoffs when he watched Clement and me call the terrific seven-game second-round series between the Flyers and Penguins.

The Flyers downed the Penguins 4–1 in Game 7 on the strength of backup goalie Ken Wregget's 39 saves. Ron Hextall was declared injured and Dave "Sudsy" Settlemyre even participated in the warm-up as one of the Flyers' two goalies. A Hextall injury was always shrouded in mystery.

I certainly gave the Flyers their due because they deserved high praise for their effort. But in the final minute, I gave the Penguins the proper sendoff because this was, at the time, their best effort in the Mario Lemieux era.

Considering it was a national broadcast, it would have been unbecoming not to mention the play of Lemieux, who had scored 12 goals in the Penguins' 11 games.

But games were an emotional experience for Ed Snider and he couldn't bear to watch me heap praise on his enemies. He requested an audience with me and he told me that he didn't care about Lemieux and the Penguins. He cared about the Flyers. And if I wanted to win over fans, I should care about the Flyers too.

During the next series against Montreal, three different Flyers executives talked to me about the situation.

I didn't think there would be lasting consequences from the Flyers' disappointment. They treated me well, particularly when I was diagnosed with cancer. Ed Snider didn't call me in on the carpet again. But that might have been a function of the fact that the Flyers had stopped making the playoffs, even after they secured Eric Lindros. They missed the playoffs for the next four years of my contract.

The first indication of the lasting consequences of that first season came in the fourth season when ESPN tried to hire Bill Clement full time. ESPN offered him a hefty raise, but he wanted to stay with the Flyers.

We were at a preseason game at Atlanta's Omni, and I had to go to the morning skate by myself because Bill was in a meeting with his agent Art Kaminsky and Flyers management.

"I don't want to go," Bill told them. "Extend me, and I stay. I want to raise my kids here."

The Flyers told Clement they thought he should move on.

He was shocked. I was shocked. I thought the Flyers' hardline approach with Clement showed they regretted giving us such lucrative contracts. They were trying to save money again.

At the start of my final year, at the opening game in Pittsburgh, the Flyers approached me and told me: "Don't worry about a thing."

I was told Gary Dornhoefer would be my partner and assured the Flyers "would make it right."

Nothing happened all season, and I still naively thought we would get a deal done. I didn't believe the Flyers were employing stall tactics. But at some point, we were pushing them about an extension, and they said they were not bringing me back.

I didn't call the media or lash out in any way. Not my style. I always try to keep it positive. I don't see the value in being negative.

The Flyers brought back Gene Hart, but the reboot only lasted one season. They allowed him to do occasional features and Jim Jackson was hired as the main TV announcer. He's still there today.

On balance, though my last experience with the Flyers left me in shock and disappointed, they had given me my first NHL opportunity, had found a place for me after the rights to Devils games had left MSG Network, and I won't forget Jay Snider's kindness when I was diagnosed with cancer.

Not surprisingly, the Flyers had hoped that Joyce would stay with the team in the ticket office. Always people who loved small towns, Joyce and I enjoyed the sense of community we found in Hershey. Because the Flyers' farm team was there, I was always five minutes from being able to see Philadelphia prospects at historic Hersheypark Arena. We never minded the 94-mile commute to Philadelphia. On game days, we would be up at 5:30 AM, out the door by 7:00, fighting rush-hour traffic for two-plus hours to make sure I got there in time for the morning skate. We'd drive home after the game. Those were very long days. If the Flyers played games on consecutive days, then we would stay in a hotel to make our lives easier.

What the Flyers didn't know was that Joyce had already worked her last day for the team, one that came months before the Flyers told me they weren't retaining my services as a broadcaster.

Joyce's last day with the Flyers was March 13, 1993, a day when a blizzard hit the area. The Flyers happened to play Wayne Gretzky and the Los Angeles Kings that day. The game was stopped after the first period. Flyers center Al Conroy scored his first NHL goal in that lone period but it wouldn't count. Joyce and I were lucky to escape the Spectrum's parking lot. Every car was buried in snow. We made no attempt to travel home to Hershey. We crept along the icy roads and skidded into the Philadelphia Airport Marriott parking lot.

Still snowbound the next day, we received a call from family telling us that Joyce's stepfather was hospitalized in Port Huron after suffering a heart attack. As soon as the runways were cleared, we caught a flight to Detroit.

Once home, Joyce discovered her stepfather needed bypass surgery and her mother was in the early stages of suffering from Alzheimer's disease, although she had not yet been diagnosed. Joyce decided to stay in Michigan to help her.

While I was back in Philadelphia waiting for a contract offer that never came, Joyce was dealing, by herself, with the torment of caring for a loved one with dementia. Not until I dropped in for a short-term stay did I realize how punishing that disease is for caregivers. She soldiered on with little complaint.

It soon became clear that she wasn't going to be able to return to her job.

The breakup didn't create lasting tension. The Flyers saw it as a business decision. After I recovered from the shock of not being renewed and started to enjoy the atmosphere of my new team, I discovered that life goes on quite well.

I didn't see Ed Snider again until we both were chosen to enter the U.S. Hockey Hall of Fame in 2011. Ed seemed genuinely glad to see me and said some very complimentary words about me at the press conference and during the induction ceremony.

After we delivered our speeches, we all sat on stools on the stage in alphabetical order. You wouldn't think that Emrick would be next to Snider, but the 2011 class included Chris Chelios, Emrick, Snider, Gary Suter, and Keith Tkachuk.

That meant we sat next to each other and talked about our days together. No mention was made by either of us about my last contract. I wouldn't have wanted it any other way.

In 1935, Alexander Graham Bell, inventor and patent holder of the first telephone, was quoted as saying: "When one door closes, another opens; but we often look so long and so regretfully upon the closed door that we do not see the one which has opened for us."

When the door slammed shut in Philly, I looked for my door opening elsewhere and found it almost immediately with SportsChannel New York doing Devils games.

In my first stint in New Jersey, they were a losing team.

By 1993, Lou Lamoriello had been in place for five years and, in his role as president and general manager, had changed the culture to that of a winner.

Thanks to flat-out blind luck, my arrival coincided with Lou's hiring of Jacques Lemaire as head coach, Larry Robinson as assistant coach, and the promotion of a kid from the AHL's Utica Devils to play goal: Martin Brodeur. Imposing defenseman Scott Stevens was named captain the previous year. Today, those five men are all in the Hockey Hall of Fame.

In that fall of 1993, the Devils won the first seven games out of the blocks.

And, as I was to see over the next 18 seasons, there was a level of excellence that was only a dream of Dr. John McMullen's when he brought the franchise to New Jersey from Denver.

I recall him telling me during that summer of 1982 the difficulty he was having in overcoming the animosity of religious groups. A devout Catholic, McMullen did not understand how people could accuse him of fostering an NHL team with a "satanic" name.

"Don't they understand? It's the Pine Barrens. It's the legend of the Devil and the Pine Barrens," he'd say.

In folklore, the Jersey Devil was a creature said to inhabit an area of southern New Jersey.

The Devils won three Stanley Cups, the first two with Dr. McMullen as owner. Brodeur became the winningest goalie in NHL history.

My time with the Devils was life-altering. The fans treated me with affection. My friendship with the Devils' fan club has extended beyond my tenure with the team. Each time I am presented with an honor of any kind, I receive a congratulatory letter from the club. They have given me honorary lifetime membership. I have been invited to speak at their meetings each year since 1983; most years, I have been able to.

Though I worked for the network that carried the team's games and not the team itself, Lou saw to it that all of us on the telecasts got Stanley Cup rings. My brother has one, my nephew another, and I kept the last one (2003). When I left, Lou supervised the team's gift, a new Lincoln. I still have it. It works wonderfully.

PULLING AN
ALL-NIGHTER

Modere "Mud" Bruneteau's most famous sports moment came near the end of the Great Depression, and yet many National Hockey League broadcasters can recite the details as if they occurred yesterday.

Rookie Bruneteau made his name synonymous with overtime hockey on March 24, 1936, when he scored at 16:30 of the sixth overtime to give the Detroit Red Wings a 1–0 win against the Montreal Maroons to end the longest playoff game in NHL history.

This one game lasted the length of three games. It ended at 2:25 AM. Players saw fans sleeping in the stands. Bruneteau's own brother Ed, listening to the game on the radio, later admitted he missed the call of his brother's goal against Lorne Chabot after he turned off the broadcast because he couldn't take the tension.

More than 80 years after Bruneteau's goal, 38 years after his death, we still talk about it. When any NHL game stretches beyond one overtime period, Bruneteau's name comes up in the press box and on the broadcast. A mention of Bruneteau is often followed by nervous laughter because it is a reminder that players and members of the media never know how long their workday will last in the playoffs.

When Easter Saturday night turned into Easter Sunday in 1987, I was in the Bruneteau zone.

Working for ESPN as the broadcaster for a Game 7 playoff game between the New York Islanders and Washington Capitals, I could see the signs that this game might go into the night.

Veteran referee Andy Van Hellemond retired his whistle early in this game. He was reluctant to provide either team a power-play opportunity. That's the way veteran referees officiated in those days. It was almost as if there was a gentleman's agreement that referees would allow players to decide tight playoff games. Most coaches and players preferred it that way.

Van Hellemond presented the Capitals with one power-play opportunity in the first period and another in the second. In the spirit of fairness, he gave the Islanders a power-play chance 1:31 into the third period.

From that point on, he had no desire to see either team have a man advantage. He called coincidental minors twice in the third, and then once in the second overtime.

Evidence of his intent not to provide either side with an advantage came in the second overtime when Washington's Greg Adams speared Kelly Hrudey.

Rather than have the Islanders go on a power play, Van Hellemond issued Adams a 10-minute misconduct. The player is gone from the game, but he can be replaced on the ice. It was Van Hellemond's version of justice served, given the context of this historical game.

In that era, he had widespread support for that line of thinking.

This game epitomized why I fell in love with hockey while I was growing up in basketball-crazy Indiana. No other sport offers the blend of drama, history, athleticism, and will-to-win that hockey can put on display.

Nothing in professional sports comes close to matching the tradition associated with the pursuit of the Stanley Cup. For more than 100 years, NHL players have dedicated two months of their lives to win a Cup.

Today's players are bigger and faster, but the game is still basically the same game it was when 21-year-old Mud Bruneteau scored the most important goal of his career in his first NHL game.

A puck is still five ounces of vulcanized rubber and the net is still 4'x6'. And there are no tie games in the playoffs. No shootouts or 3-on-3, either. You play until someone scores a goal under normal conditions, even if it takes all night. In 2016–17, 27 NHL playoff games went to overtime. The league's 20-year average reveals that about 23 percent of all NHL postseason games require overtime. The symbol of the NHL playoffs is a bleary-eyed fan trying to navigate through his or her workday after watching late-night overtimes.

Hockey players are skillful, but the playoffs are less about skill and more about endurance, overcoming physical challenges, and determination. The NHL playoffs are the equivalent of running a gauntlet where surviving is winning.

Many NHL players know the story of Bobby Baun, playing with a broken leg, scoring an overtime goal for the Toronto Maple Leafs against the Detroit Red Wings in the 1964 playoffs, and they all seem to attempt to live up to the standard Baun set. Playing through injuries isn't a requirement, but an expectation. In the postseason, players seem more like modern-day gladiators than athletes.

Fate has been democratic when it comes to anointing playoff overtime goal-scorers. Superstar Joe Sakic leads the all-time list with eight goals and fellow Hall of Famer Maurice "Rocket" Richard is second with six.

But the list of overtime scorers also includes lesser-known players such as Joonas Donskoi, Matt Beleskey, Dale Weise, Bryan Bickell, Brian Skrudland, Travis Moen, Nikolai Borschevky, Dave Hannan, Todd Gill, and Brad May, among others.

Bruneteau was the youngest player on the ice the night he became an NHL legend. He had been promoted from the International Hockey League just two weeks before.

Before the Easter Epic, the longest game I had ever broadcast was a double-overtime contest when I was with the American League's Maine Mariners. But I was prepared for whatever was going to come my way. I once heard famed baseball broadcaster Red Barber say to always go to the bathroom before every game, whether you need to go or not, because you never know how long you are going to be on the air. Always followed Barber's advice.

The Capital Centre didn't have broadcast booths. Four different television networks were broadcasting this game, including both the Capitals' and Islanders' home networks. That's the way it was done back then. Our broadcasting booth consisted of an eight-foot banquet table, the kind you would see at a Knights of Columbus, Moose, or VFW hall, that was set up in the lower concourse area. There was a gap in the seats, and our table was placed there. We were supposed to sit on a cement abutment behind the table.

But our producer, Bryan Cooper, inspected the site before the game and concluded we needed cushions. He went to a local mall and purchased two Washington Redskins seat cushions, one for me and one for my analyst, Bill Clement. I can tell you that the game would have been a pain in our backsides without those cushions.

Don't recall precisely when Bill and I knew we were in a historical game, but it became obvious that the players were sensing the epic nature of the contest. They began to focus more on not losing, making the safer play rather than daring effort that might lead to a critical mistake.

It is never easy to play mistake-free hockey, particularly when fatigue is undermining your efforts more than your opponent. Through the first overtime, the two teams had combined for 79 shots. The goalies, Bob Mason (Washington Capitals) and Kelly Hrudey (New York

Islanders), weighed down by sweat-drenched equipment, may have had the biggest challenge on this night.

No cell phones, social media, or even Internet, in that era. But word of this game spread anyway. People who had watched the game informed me later that they called friends to ask if they were watching.

This was a game that picked up viewers as it went along. Philadelphia Flyers forward Tim Kerr, whose team would play the winner of the Islanders-Capitals series, told me later that he went to bed in the third period and then couldn't sleep because he was thinking about what he was missing. He climbed out of bed and reclaimed his place in front of his television.

In the overtime, I was starting to feel sorry for the players because you could see fatigue was having an impact.

Former Islanders player Duane Sutter told me years later that "by the time we got to the third overtime we all had enough left for one good rush and then straight to the bench."

As a broadcaster, you know that if something dramatic is going to happen in an overtime period, it is likely going to happen in the first few minutes. Game-breakers have a burst of energy coming out of an intermission, and that can carry them for a few shifts.

But after about three or four shifts, you could see shoulders drooping as they would sit on the bench. Then their focus would shift to greater emphasis on defensive play.

Sometimes players would fall, probably because of fatigue, and then you might see a player feel a rush of adrenaline and try to take advantage of the situation. But players, as a rule, play more carefully in overtime.

One reason why you see third- or fourth-line players occasionally scoring overtime goals is because they are the most rested people in the building. They aren't playing much because the coach is primarily using his best players. Sometimes they get a 20-second shift and turn it into a play fans won't ever forget.

As a broadcaster, I can relate to the ebbs and flows of energy. We also reacquire our energy during intermissions, especially in overtime, when the show goes back to the network where pre-planned features, video highlights, and analysis are offered. That's when broadcasters receive their breaks. We aren't usually involved between periods. We stretch our legs, use the bathroom, grab a bottle of water. It's our time to recharge our batteries.

But because of the length of this game, Bill and I were growing more weary than usual. Compounding the problem was the reality that the preplanned intermission features were used up. Instead of taking a break, we were engaging with ESPN studio host Tom Mees to add further insight about this game that was destined to become an instant classic.

Without our usual intermission break, we were growing more tired than usual as the game stretched beyond midnight.

At some point, can't tell you exactly when, Bill and I became slap-happy in the Easter Epic. Bill started talking about removing articles of clothes if this game continued much longer. His shirt and tie came off in the second overtime, and he was threatening to remove his T-shirt during the third overtime.

Clement, an ex-NHL player, had done some modeling and at one point I said if the viewers wanted to see a bare-chested male model they should tune in for the third overtime period.

We were trying to have fun.

That became clear to our audience during the intermission between the second and third overtime period when Mees brought us in to discuss what was happening on the ice. That's not exactly what we did.

The segment is available on YouTube. What you see is Bill, minus his dress shirt and with a tie wrapped around his head like a Native American headband. I had not gone as far as Bill, but my shirt was unbuttoned and my tie was undone.

Mees couldn't contain his amusement.

"Let's go back live to the Cap Centre," Mees said, laughing at the sight. "Get a load of Bill Clement. I didn't know, Mike Emrick, that you had the chief of the Apache Nation with you."

"This is Cochise, son of Grilled Cheese," I said. "Right out of a John Wayne western saga. Duke, what do you think?"

Bill had an assortment of impressions he could perform on cue, and it was my job to tee it up for him.

"I thought the game was yesterday and here it is Easter today," Clement said, with a Wayne impersonation that was right on the money.

Fortunately, or unfortunately, we weren't done with our silliness. I teed it up again for Clement.

"What are your impressions of the game?" I asked. "Do someone else. Do Boom Boom Geoffrion."

At the time, the Montreal Canadiens legend Geoffrion had added notoriety from appearing in Miller Lite commercials. Bill used an exaggerated French Canadian accent, something befitting the movie *Slap Shot*, and said we were witnessing "one of the greatest hockey games ever in the history of the National Hockey League."

Clement was comfortable performing in front of a camera. After playing 719 games in the NHL with the Philadelphia Flyers, Washington Capitals, and Atlanta and Calgary Flames, from 1971 to 1982, Clement had worked as a male model and then trained to be an actor.

131

The year before this game, Clement had a role on the ABC daytime drama *All My Children*. He also had appeared in many commercials. He knew what he had to do to give people a late-night laugh.

After being a hardworking role player, Clement became a hardworking performer. He was masterful at preparing for a pregame introduction. He'd go off in the corner, think about what he was going to say, and then come back and deliver it perfectly.

We were attempting to inject some fun into this classic, but not everyone enjoyed our comedy improv.

When I returned from a trip to bathroom, I found Clement back in shirt, tie, and jacket.

"We got a call, didn't we?" I asked.

In hindsight, I still don't have any regrets about our attempt to add humor to this game.

Leave it to Clement to perfectly explain our performance that night.

"If you aren't willing to step out on the ledge during your career," Bill said, "then you will remain a slice of white bread on the sandwich of life. No multigrain, no pumpernickel, no rye."

In an interview specifically for this book, Clement said even today, more than three decades after this game, he still has people say to him in airports, restaurants, or public appearances, "Hey, Bill, when are you going to tie a tie around your head again?"

This was the first full season that Clement and I had worked together, and he believes this memorable game "put us on the map."

Clement has said more than once that the drama of the game, with its twists and turns, was a perfect vehicle for me to showcase my ability. I don't know if that was the case, but I do know it was a fun game to call.

"There were very few people who didn't have fun with us as we were doing it," Clement said. "We weren't being critical of either team. We weren't going out on a limb with things we were saying about the game. We were two guys having fun with an incredible event that was so enjoyable."

What we didn't know at the time is that we would have another 28-plus minutes of play before we would determine a winner.

Players said afterward that they struggled to deal with the fatigue that came from playing a game that was hockey's version of a doubleheader.

Washington Capitals goalie Bob Mason told me later that he lost 14 pounds in the game, and it might have been a higher total had he not eaten oranges between periods.

Hunger was an issue for the players. It has been reported that the Islanders ordered pizzas during the overtime and some players consumed a slice or two.

New York Islanders goalie Kelly Hrudey told me that players tried to keep the mood light by telling bad jokes during the intermissions and found themselves laughing uncontrollably, more at their teammates' feeble attempts at joke-telling than the jokes themselves.

They are athletes, not comedians, and the weariness they were experiencing caused them to stumble over words and destroy punchlines.

As the Easter Epic stretched through the first, second, and third overtime and finally into the fourth, it was as if what happened to get there was washed away. It's almost forgotten today that Bryan Trottier scored with 5:23 left in regulation to force bonus hockey.

This was a quality game even before it arrived in overtime. At one point in the third period, I said on the broadcast: "How many faceoffs have been [Bryan] Trottier vs. [Mike] Ridley, 50? Sixty?"

It would have been a classic Game 7 even if it had ended after 60 minutes.

Years later, in an article published by the *Hockey News*, Mason admitted that he broke his skate on the Trottier goal. A rivet snapped on the heel of his Lange skate. Nothing could be done until the intermission. That means Mason played the last five minutes of regulation on one functional skate.

In the first overtime, Washington's Greg Smith flew a shot past Hrudey, but it clanged off the right post and caromed harmlessly away.

Players didn't stop playing physical, not even in overtime. Washington's rugged defenseman Scott Stevens crushed New York forward Pat Flatley with a stunning open-ice hit in the second overtime.

"I thought he killed him," Clement said in the same *Hockey News* article. Clement compared the hit to Stevens' famed hit against Eric Lindros except "with less damage."

When the game moved into the fourth overtime, it was the NHL's first four-overtime game in 36 years.

Players were exhausted. Pat LaFontaine said in an NHL.com article that he asked his trainer for oxygen before the fourth overtime. He has also said he remembers the theme song from *The Twilight Zone* playing over the speakers in the fourth overtime. Clement also recalls that moment, offering that it reinforced to him that others realized how bizarre this game had become.

We had entered another dimension in sports, a dimension not only of sight and sound, but of mind. And it was a journey into a wondrous land of imagination.

The whole night seemed surreal and the ending was a tale of the unexpected.

After a shot from Kenny Leiter went wide, Gord Dineen claimed the puck behind the net. He brought it out front and tried to drive it home, but the puck was blocked and deflected out to the point.

LaFontaine, a dynamic offensive player who usually would be at the net, was only at the point because he was covering up for Dineen.

The puck came at an odd angle, and LaFontaine had to spin before firing the puck toward the net. Because the puck was on its side when LaFontaine struck, it knuckled toward the net.

Mason was screened on the play by Islanders player Dale Henry and Langway. LaFontaine's drive touched Washington defenseman Kevin Hatcher's stick and deflected. I can remember hearing the puck strike the iron of the net and then saw the rubber disc drop into the net.

My call: "Turn around. Pat LaFontaine. Scoooorrrreeeee!"

A clean, succinct call. That's the way I prefer it. I don't rehearse lines or have catchphrases.

I've been asked over the years about the many words I use to describe the movement of the puck. The truth is, those are just words that come to mind. When I was in grad school, someone in the IHL advised me to come up with different ways of saying the same thing, lest you find yourself saying the puck has been "dumped" in over and over. There's also an old saying that a broadcaster should never use words longer than "marmalade." Hopefully the words I use are not foreign to most people.

Former International Hockey League referee Sam Sisco used to tell me that the hope of all referees in overtime is that the game ends on a goal without controversy. No disturbances. No confusion. No doubt a goal was scored. That works for broadcasters as well. Just have the correct goal-scorer. Describe the moment. Let the picture on the screen speak for itself. That's my approach.

What I remember about the moment was how quiet the building was in the seconds after LaFontaine scored. Remember, the Islanders won this game in Landover, Maryland. Fans had been sitting for more than six hours only to watch their team lose. This was a sober crowd. Concession sales had been cut off hours before. They sat in stunned silence.

You could hear the New York players squealing all over the building. Mason seemed frozen in place. Many of the Capitals milled about as if they didn't know what to do or say.

After the game, Mees came back to us for a wrap-up. What I said was: "There were three games in the National Hockey League tonight and they were all here."

Hrudey's statistics said more than I could: he made 73 saves in a game that lasted six hours and 18 minutes. After he surrendered one to Washington's Grant Martin, he made 50 stops without giving up a goal. Included in that stretch were 17 saves in the second overtime.

After the game, Hrudey was dismayed to learn that his six-hour VHS tape, normally more than capable of recording an NHL game, had not captured the last half hour of the contest. He could not have guessed that the game would end at 1:58 AM. We were eventually able to provide him a tape of the extra action.

Mason finished with 54 saves, but that wasn't enough on this night.

As Bill and I left the Cap Centre, we happened upon three members of a wedding party, dressed in tuxedos, who had managed to work their way down near the Islanders bus. They told us they had traveled from New York for the nuptials. They participated in the wedding ceremony, drove to the Cap Centre to watch some of the action, returned to the reception, and were stunned to discover the game was still ongoing as the festivities were winding down. With ticket stubs still in hand, they hustled to the arena in time to see LaFontaine's memorable goal.

Hunger was the overriding sensation once Bill and I were outside the arena. The only restaurant open was a nearby Denny's. When we showed up, the line to get a seat stretched out the door. We were both tired and looking forward to discussing what we had just witnessed. It never occurred to us that the bars in the D.C. area had just emptied and everyone in town seemed to be in search of an early Easter breakfast. The place was packed, and many of the folks had been at the game or watched it on ESPN.

An hour after the game, the adrenaline was still flowing and the natural tendency is to replay your performance in your mind. You second-guess what you said or didn't say. Folks in the restaurant had told us that our impromptu comedy show in the overtime intermission had played well, but we were less sure of that. The reviews from ESPN executives had yet to be received.

We were right to be concerned. *USA Today* television critic Rachel Shuster interviewed ESPN vice president Loren Matthews, who questioned our decision to try a Vaudeville act in place of a standard intermission interview. He wasn't happy. That was Shuster's storyline in Monday's newspaper.

But when I was home in Cherry Hill, New Jersey, the next day, the doorbell sounded, and a delivery person gave me a box that contained a bottle of Dom Perignon champagne.

The card was from ESPN president J. William Grimes, and it read: "I know there is such a thing as decorum. Nevertheless…"

Today, the Easter Epic ranks as the 10th-longest game in NHL history. Since that night, five other games have gone longer, none coming close to moving past the length of the Mud Bruneteau game in 1936, or even the 1933 game when the Maple Leafs downed the

Boston Bruins 1–0 on a goal by Ken Doraty at 4:46 of the sixth overtime. The longest game since then was a five-overtime thriller with Keith Primeau scoring to give the Flyers a 2–1 win against the Pittsburgh Penguins in 2000.

But even at No. 10, the Easter Epic is known as one of the most memorable games in NHL history.

Clement has called this game "the Woodstock of hockey."

"No one realized what they were getting into when they arrived," Clement said. "But at some point, they realized, 'Holy, cow, we are witnessing history here.'"

People ask me to rank the best games I've ever had the privilege of broadcasting and the best I can do is give them a top 10. The Sidney Crosby Winter Classic goal at Ralph Wilson Stadium in Buffalo in 2008 is among them, as is the game when Martin Brodeur became the winningest goalie in NHL history. I would also include the 1998 U.S. women's gold medal triumph in Nagano, Japan. This game has a permanent place on the list because it sums up everything I love about the sport.

Another would be T.J. Oshie's marathon shootout performance to help the 2014 U.S. Olympic team defeat Russia in Sochi. When NHL play resumed back in the States, I saw Oshie after the morning skate when he and the Blues were in Chicago for a game with the Blackhawks.

"I noticed that during those six consecutive shootout attempts, you had a smile on your face each time you picked up the puck," I began. "Why?"

Oshie grinned. "Well, it was getting kinda funny," he said.

I wouldn't have seen it that way if I had been nervously holding that stick. But that's why he's one of the best there is when it comes to shootouts.

I asked, "Was that the best thing that ever happened to you in your life?"

"No," he said, smiling. "Just after we got back home, my first child was born. That was awesome."

Skill alone wasn't enough to win this playoff game. The Islanders needed survival skills to emerge victorious. Perseverance, stamina, and will were prerequisites for success in this game. It's a game I will never forget.

SIDEKICKS

BILL CLEMENT

When my eyes opened in a darkened room, the day after cancer surgery, the first people I saw were my grinning partner Bill Clement and producer Bryan Cooper sitting in chairs near my bed.

They had driven to Baltimore's Johns Hopkins Hospital from nearby Landover, Maryland, where the Flyers had played the night before, with the dedicated purpose of being there for my first sign of coherency.

Not sure what time it was. Maybe it was 6:00 AM, perhaps 7:00, undoubtedly before visitors were allowed on the floor. Clement and Cooper were young, wearing suits, and confident enough to breeze past the nurse's station. I would guess the Johns Hopkins staff assumed they were interns.

I don't recall what the guys said to me, although I'm confident there was wisecracking about me being laid out in a hospital gown. But the important element of this story is that they were there for me.

Throughout my career, the one common theme among the handful of color analysts that have partnered with me is that they have been talented. But more importantly, they've been quality people. In every case, we have become good friends.

Clement was a natural as a color commentator, a trained performer, rich in insight and humor. He could boil down critical analysis to a concise, glib line that would leave you laughing and thinking at the same time.

Baseball's best hitters can hit whatever you throw at them. That's how Clement is as an analyst. You throw anything at him during a broadcast and he will get good wood on it. Often, he will hit it out of the park.

It was 1986 when Clement and I started to work together for MSG Network. He was hired as Sal Messina's backup, meaning Bill worked the Devils telecast when Sal had New York Rangers conflicts.

Clement was an immediate hit. Because he was in the New York market, ESPN discovered him quickly. Thus began his long run at ESPN. Our ESPN pairing lasted two years and we worked together four years with the Flyers.

It wasn't hard to understand why Clement made it to the NHL as a role player: he has always worked to improve himself. He did it as a hockey player, an actor, and even as an analyst.

We held our own "training camp," practicing on camera, sharpening our interview style. We'd record it, play it back, and analyze our work. We'd discuss what to do and what not to do. We even coordinated our blue blazers and ties to make sure we looked like a team on camera.

People would say, "Do you know you are wearing the same ties?"

"Yes," we would say, and they would look at us funny.

Not everyone understood what we were doing. But it worked for us. It was perfect for me. I had come from radio and didn't have much television in my background. I was thrilled to have someone who worked as hard at his craft as Clement did.

When I was diagnosed with cancer, I had a much better understanding of what former Penguins coach Red Kelly meant when he said "you can count on one hand" the friends who stay with you during rough seas.

When I became ill, Bill was a rock. He was also there for me when Joyce had a health scare. And he shared my joy when it passed. He helped prop me up when I was fired.

You don't forget friends like Clement. I don't see him as often anymore, but what I miss more than anything is his comedy, particularly his impressions. One of my favorites is the depiction of a police officer making an arrest on an interstate highway. He can do it in a variety of dialects. He does impressions of everyone from John Wayne to Popeye to almost all of his old coaches.

Whatever he did, I laughed in response. I'm easily amused. When I see him again, I will ask him to do all my favorite impressions. And I will laugh again.

SAL MESSINA

I've worked with many hardworking people during my career, but none of them worked harder than my New York Rangers broadcast partner Sal Messina.

He did every Rangers game on the radio. No exceptions. And his real job was selling airline parts.

Think about that. While on the road in Winnipeg, Los Angeles, and Vancouver, Sal kept up with his sales calls. While I went to the morning skate in Chicago, he would be visiting a client at the O'Hare or Midway airports.

Before I worked for Madison Square Garden, Sal also served as the Rangers' spare goalie. In the Original Six era, teams wouldn't have a second goalie on the roster. He never got into an NHL game, but he told me he came very close one night in Montreal when Rangers netminder Jacques Plante suffered an asthma attack. Sal was in full gear, ready to go, when Plante walked into the dressing room and announced: "I'll go."

I am guessing he was the most enthusiastic airplane parts salesman in the company because that was his general attitude. A terrific man with a winning personality. I was thrilled to see the Hockey Hall of Fame honor him with the Foster Hewitt Memorial Award.

Sometimes the games at MSG seemed like the Wild West when Sal and I worked together. Our broadcast location was in the crowd, in a small media box, 15 feet from the glass. We were two rows from the walkway at center ice. It was like sitting in the front row at the Indianapolis 500. Everything came flying at you and left quickly.

The MSG security guards were heavy-handed in those days, given the autonomy to keep the peace in the stands.

One night, I remember I was calling the play. Tony McKegney of the Minnesota North Stars was stickhandling deftly through center ice. No one was there to check him. A play was developing. Suddenly there was a strange sound, an audible "ooohhhhh" coming from the paying customers. The play was whistled dead. Confusion reigned.

When we went to commercial break, I removed my headset to converse with Sal.

"What happened?" I asked. "What was the crowd reaction about?"

"Oh, that," Sal deadpanned. "An usher threw a guy down the steps and he hit the boards."

Life was entertaining when Sal was with you. He is now retired and living in Florida. I think about him and often miss those days.

PETER McNAB

When analyst Peter McNab was given me as a broadcast partner with the New Jersey Devils, he inherited two situations at once.

He got a broadcaster who had just been fired (or not renewed) by the Philadelphia Flyers and the man who was replacing popular Gary Thorne, who had been his partner for seven years. Just to make that challenge more interesting, Jacques Lemaire and Larry Robinson had been hired as coach and assistant coach, respectively, and young Martin Brodeur was taking over in net.

But McNab is such a kind, jovial, hockey-loving, easygoing guy that he made it a peaceful transition of power. He "talked me off the bridge" a few times when I was having flashbacks of my Philadelphia exit.

McNab, son of former NHL player and executive Max McNab, was a second-generation NHLer who inherited his father's ability to talk hockey. He netted 363 goals in his NHL career and scored 40-plus goals twice, but doesn't mind telling you about being forced to sit as a Buffalo Sabres rookie against the Philadelphia Flyers during the 1975 Stanley Cup Final.

"My job as a young, healthy scratch was to drive goalie Roger Crozier to the rink for games," McNab said. "We would stop occasionally between his house and the arena so he could throw up into a trash basket."

Every athlete handles nervousness in his or her own way.

McNab's father played in an era when the Norris family owned three of the six teams. Max McNab was once traded by one Norris team, the Detroit Red Wings, to another Norris team, the Chicago Blackhawks. How was that even allowed?

Before he was dealt by Detroit, Max did get an opportunity to center Gordie Howe and Ted Lindsay for a brief period when Sid Abel was injured.

The McNab family history gave Peter a deeper insight.

Peter and I could not have asked for a better situation. Lamoriello, Lemaire, Robinson, and their energized Devils made our jobs fascinating every night. With Brodeur splitting the goalie duties with Chris Terreri, that energized Devils season was a 180-degree reversal from the situation I just left.

With Lemaire preaching defense, when the Devils scored two goals, it seemed like six because their defensive coverage could strangle an offense. Once the Devils showed their 1-2-2 defensive scheme, it was lights out early for their opponent.

This was an era when low scoring was a way of life. But Peter knew this wasn't the first time in league history that scoring was down.

"I remember Max would tell me," young Peter recalled, "that when Mr. Campbell would add up the scores of the games each week, if the average total goals fell below five, he would call the referees and say, 'Gentlemen, we need more power plays.'"

Peter understood earlier than the rest of us that what the Devils were doing was going to make them a superpower.

In 1995, the Devils advanced to the Stanley Cup Final against the heavily favored Detroit Red Wings. Peter and I were watching Game 2 in Detroit, preparing to do a postgame report. ESPN was broadcasting the game.

Out of the blue, Peter said: "The Devils are going to win the Stanley Cup and it might be a sweep."

I am only 5-foot-7. McNab stands 6-foot-4. I looked up at him and said, "I beg your pardon?"

He repeated the prediction. A minute or two later, New Jersey defenseman Scott Niedermayer made his famous dash to score a goal against Mike Vernon and tie the game. As McNab had foreseen, the Devils swept the series.

That series was our last time together. McNab told me as much before then, that whether the team stayed in New Jersey or moved to Nashville, which had been rumored, he was going to be joining the Quebec Nordiques in their move to Denver. McNab has been an Avalanche analyst ever since.

JOHN DAVIDSON

What made John Davidson a masterful analyst is that he could work a room without going into the room.

When I think of JD, I see him standing in the hallway outside the dressing room. It was impressive and fun to watch him work. No pen. No paper. No recorder. You'd see him chatting and laughing with everyone coming in and out of the dressing room. Equipment managers, trainers, players, coaches, assistant coaches, the general managers, all stopped to chat with JD.

Davidson was a great listener. That was his secret. And when everyone was gone, he would dart around the corner and tear three sheets from a yellow legal pad. He would write notes for the home team on one page, notes from the visiting team on the second, and the third sheet was reserved for news from around the league.

Before the game started, he would spread his three papers on the tabletop of our broadcast booth. He would inform the broadcast truck which players he planned to talk about, to give producers a chance to have video or graphics ready during a stoppage in play. Davidson was a broadcasting marvel, a yardstick by which other analysts could measure themselves.

"Everybody reads the Internet if they're fans," Davidson said. "I've got to have fresh items every day on both teams."

His news was always fresh. And he never went hunting for information without bagging his limit.

The last season John and I worked together, in 2005–06, he worked 153 games and I worked 152. That included men's and women's hockey at the Olympics in Torino, Italy; our preseason and regular season games (Davidson for the New York Rangers and me for the Devils); NBC regular season games and playoffs; and OLN regular season games.

Our lengthy season finally came to an end in Raleigh, North Carolina, when Mr. Game 7, Justin Williams, scored into an empty net, giving the Hurricanes their first Stanley Cup over the Edmonton Oilers.

We signed off, grabbed the elevator down from the press box, and left out of the loading dock door. We had ordered a car to be waiting for us in the parking lot. The problem was no one had left the game. The parking lot was full. Everyone was in the building watching the celebration. With so many cars still there, we couldn't find our ride.

Davidson is 6-foot-3 and I can picture him walking down the aisles craning his neck with the hope of spotting a limousine with its lights on.

We started laughing because no matter how well we planned our escape from an arena, it was always delayed.

We finally found the car and fled the parking lot before the fans filed out. What we didn't know at the time was that game would be our last working together. Davidson decided to make a career switch by becoming president of the St. Louis Blues. From there, he moved to the Columbus Blue Jackets, and now he's in charge of the New York Rangers. He clearly made the right decision.

I'm left with a long list of fond memories about working with Davidson. I loved his stories, especially the ones about his former goalie partner Gilles Gratton, who believed he was reincarnated.

Gratton said in a previous life he was a count who stoned people to death, and that's why he was a goalie in this life. He also said he was killed during the Spanish Inquisition by being run through by a lance.

"On game day," Davidson said, "our coach, John Ferguson, would walk into the dressing room at the morning skate and toss a puck to that night's starting goalie. Then he would leave. If he tossed it to me, Gratton went into a big celebration dance. If he tossed it to Gilles, he would pretend he was having a heart attack."

Gratton apparently had interest in astrology, once saying he couldn't play because the moon was in the wrong place in the sky.

Davidson told me that after a bad start, Gratton once pulled himself from the game by skating to the bench and saying: "It's not in the stars tonight, Fergie."

Perhaps my favorite Davidson story came during a pre–Stanley Cup media session, when we were asked about how much money players earn in the playoffs. I said something about players not really concerning themselves with that.

Davidson was able to amplify my point with a memorable personal story about the New York Rangers reaching the Stanley Cup Final with him in the net in 1979.

"The city of New York went crazy," Davidson said. "It was a thrilling run for all of us. So, the smoke clears. A couple weeks later, I went to the front door and the mail was there and I'm sorting through it and there was an envelope from the National Hockey League."

Davidson said he had no idea why the NHL was sending him anything.

"I opened it up," Davidson said. "It was a check—my playoff share. I forgot we got paid."

GLENN "CHICO" RESCH

I often have said that God put Chico in my life to help me at a time when he knew I needed it the most.

Resch helped me find humility, to understand that I shouldn't take myself too seriously, to comfort me when both of my parents died, and to be with me when we lost our dear sweet dog.

By the time Resch and his wife got to know Joyce and me, we were already living in Michigan. MSG did not require that we live in New Jersey. Joyce had retired from her job with the Flyers and gone back to Michigan to take care of her parents. It just made sense for us to live in Michigan.

But despite how far we lived apart, I always knew Resch and his wife would be there for us.

Once while we were all grumbling about a flight delay and Chico still had a smile on his face, former New Jersey Devils beat writer Kara Yorio called him "the most consistently positive person I've ever seen."

That was a succinct description of Resch. Plus, he brought an overall faith to his positive attitude. That's why I believe there was "an unseen hand" making sure we were able to spend many years together.

We had fun together when we were Devils broadcasters from 1996 to 2011. There was an informality to our broadcasts. Don't confuse that with a lack of professionalism; it was just a homey approach. Not everyone liked it, but many did.

One of our nightly features, called "Chico Eats," showed Resch sampling the fare at a different food stand in the new Newark arena. Encouraged by our producer Roland Dratch, T-shirts with checkmark boxes were created for fans to show they had eaten where Resch had been in our segments.

We had a stuffed animal named Chuck the Duck who had a cigar in his mouth. He would appear on intermission segments.

More importantly, the Devils were winning. It was enjoyable to come to work and find everyone on the team feeling positive about their lives.

Resch is a former NHL goalie who ended his career playing with the Devils and Flyers. I knew him before we were broadcast partners.

Whenever his analysis favored the goaltender, I would jokingly tell him that he was being nice to a goalie fraternity brother, or words to that effect. But Resch's knowledge of the goaltending position added insider knowledge to our telecast. He could tell viewers when a goal was a goalie's fault and when it wasn't. Resch had stopped more than 15,000 shots in a career that included a three-season run at Minnesota-Duluth, a season in the IHL, time in the AHL and the Central Hockey League, plus 14 NHL seasons.

He played for the Muskegon Mohawks in 1971–72, before I was calling games for the Port Huron Flags. But he played for coach Moose Lallo, one of my childhood heroes.

Resch tells a great story about holding out for an extra $50 per week when he was playing for the Mohawks. He was making $250 per week and wanted $300. The Mohawks didn't cave on that until their other goalie showed up overweight to training camp.

Lallo had a lot of team rules in those days, and one was players couldn't eat pancakes. Lallo believed pancakes were bad for digestion and conditioning.

One night, Resch was in net when the Mohawks beat the Fort Wayne Komets on the road and the team stopped for dinner afterward. The chosen restaurant was, of all places, the International House of Pancakes.

Having beaten the system once on his contract, Resch decided to tempt fate a second time.

"I want the blueberry pancakes," Resch whispered to the waitress. "But if the guy in the brown trench coat is watching, don't bring them to me."

The plan failed. The pancakes arrived at Resch's table; Lallo arrived a moment later.

"Resch," Lallo said, wagging his finger. "Those pancakes better taste good cuz they're going to cost you $50."

It probably wasn't a coincidence that $50 was the fine Lallo assessed.

But my favorite Resch story involves the lucky elephant dung. Some hockey players are superstitious, and Resch was one who believed in what legendary Hall of Fame coach Dick Irvin called the "unseen hand."

The hand was the invisible force that often changes the course of a game. During his playing days, Resch's glove hand was more valuable to him than the unseen hand. But he was willing to go along with any superstition, just in case it would help.

In 1975, when Resch's New York Islanders were playing the New York Rangers in a first-round playoff series, they had to share Madison Square Garden with circus animals. Ringling Brothers was at the "World's Most

Famous Arena" for an extended stay and somehow became important to the series.

"Someone got the idea that what the elephants were leaving behind was good luck," Resch said.

Yep. The Islanders began to believe in the power of elephant poop. Good luck dung, as it were.

The elephant dung was shoveled into garbage bags (hopefully double-bagged). Belief in the dung grew stronger when the Islanders dispatched the Rangers in the first round. They had a fresh supply when they rallied from an 0–3 series deficit to take down the Penguins.

When preparing for road games, the bagged dung was loaded into the bus' storage compartment.

The Islanders believed the elephant dung was still working when they rallied from an 0–3 deficit to force a Game 7 in the third round against the Flyers. The Force and feces were with them when they traveled to Philadelphia for the deciding game.

But teams and bagged elephant dung can lose their power over time. Would guess the Islanders dumped their dung somewhere near Broad Street on their way out of town.

Five years later, the Islanders won their first Stanley Cup and no elephant dung was involved, as far as we know.

EDDIE

Eddie O likes to joke that when he was a young teen in a Catholic school that he was always "catching the yardstick" because a nun or priest would spy a badly hidden racing form peeking out of his bookbag.

Once I got to know him well and understood his passion for the horses, I realized he wasn't joking.

Olczyk was a 20-goal NHL scorer at 18 and generated 90 points for the Maple Leafs in 1988–89. But his ability as a horse handicapper is equally impressive. He dazzled the NBC hockey broadcast crew on 2013 Kentucky Derby Day when he accurately predicted, on air, the top four finishers three hours before the race.

Shortly thereafter, it was announced Olczyk the hockey guy would be joining the Derby Day crew at Churchill Downs. He's been a fixture at Triple Crown races and other Thoroughbred events ever since.

It's an impressive sidelight for man who happens to be exceptional at his regular job as lead analyst on NBC's hockey coverage. He has keen insight on how a team is performing and he's an eagle eye on deflections. He has dependable instincts on who to trust.

But you have to understand that Eddie is going to be drawn to the ponies from time to time. Once, when we were working the Western Conference Final for NHL Radio, we went to a baseball game in Denver on an off day during an Avalanche–Red Wings series. Suddenly, Eddie disappeared midgame. He went to the track with director of officiating Andy Van Hellemond. Talk about mixing business with pleasure.

He likes to say he turned me into a gambler, but I went willingly and not for very much money.

On Wednesday, December 4, 2013, we were sitting in the broadcast booth at Detroit's Joe Louis Arena when we noticed the Red Wings had joined the other league teams with a 50-50 raffle.

Between the second and third period, I nudged Eddie and pointed to the scoreboard, which showed the raffle was at $24,000.

Before I could say anything, Eddie shoved his hand in his pocket and pulled out two $20 bills. He gave them to our NBC runner Kim and asked her to buy tickets right away. I offered him $20 for my half.

"No, no," Eddie said. "I've got this one. We're in."

You always remember where you were when something magical happens. I remember describing Henrik Zetterberg carrying the puck down the right-wing offensive boards. Plenty of Flyers back on defense.

Not an unusual or potentially dangerous play. But out of the corner of my eye, I spy Eddie's arms pumping up and down. Shortly after, we had a commercial break.

"We won! We won!" he said.

With the take of a nearly $30,000 gross, we won a little under $15,000!

Kim headed down to the Red Wings offices with our strip of numbers and Eddie's driver's license.

It took six weeks, but he received the cash. Eddie gave Kim $500 for being the runner. He gave Uncle Sam $5,000 for being the country that fostered the freedom to compete in the 50-50. He and I both received $4,950.

I'd like to say that, in later 50-50s, we still had a lot of that $4,950 each remaining. Too many years of coming up empty in Detroit and Pittsburgh and New York and Philadelphia and Chicago have passed. It's called gambling for a reason.

I always say that my job is always enjoyable when you like the person you are on the air with. That's Eddie, as a person and an analyst.

He is as likeable as they come. I will never forget the first time I met him. I knew he had been picked for the U.S. Olympic team at 16 and played at 17 and was now an American playing for the Toronto Maple Leafs. That couldn't have been easy.

One morning in the late 1980s, I was with the Flyers at Maple Leaf Gardens, standing with Gene Hart and other media members who were gathered around Leafs owner Harold Ballard in the arena's lower bowl. Ballard was viewed as the Mr. Scrooge of the hockey world. He was crotchety, a true curmudgeon, but he was never boring. When he opened his mouth, reporters gathered. His observations about the game were always considered news, or at least something we could laugh about.

During the impromptu press conference, we could see Eddie Olczyk bounding up the stairs with noticeable enthusiasm to pay respects to his team's owner.

Arriving at the top of the stairs, Eddie shook hands with us all, including Ballard, who was sitting in a wheelchair. Eddie bowed his head a bit to get closer to his boss.

"Just want to say I like being here with the team," he told Ballard.

What player goes out of his way to pay respects to his owner? We later learned that Olczyk greeted Ballard on a regular basis. Even when he was a 42-goal scorer, Olczyk never took his job for granted.

The Olczyk boys grew up working in their dad's grocery store—Edmar Foods—and they worked hard.

"'Clean up in Aisle 6' usually meant a bunch of cracked and broken baby food jars," Olczyk remembered.

Through the years, I have gotten to know the Olczyk family. Everyone in the family is good-looking. Even the dogs. The Olczyk children, now adults, are always polite to their elders. It's been fun to watch the children grow up and to see the love the family has for each other and other people.

When John Davidson left broadcasting for St. Louis' presidency, NBC determined Bill Clement would be their guy for the studio. Eddie was a familiar name and face. He was chosen to sit in the chair next to me. We've only grown closer through the years. I'm a cancer survivor. He's a cancer survivor. That has just strengthened a bond that was already tight.

At our first meeting, Eddie told me: "I'll always have your back, Doc."

That was 2006. I was 59. He took me through my 60s and now into my 70s. And he has always kept that vow.

9

HEIDI RETURNS
AS *MRS. DOUBTFIRE*

It's impossible to know precisely when football became such a focal point of America's sports landscape. But we can pinpoint when we truly understood that football was more important than we realized.

That came on November 17, 1968, when NBC inexplicably interrupted an AFL game between the Oakland Raiders and New York Jets to show the movie *Heidi* about a girl living in the Swiss Alps.

NBC executives wished they could hide in the Swiss Alps after the plug was pulled on a three-point game in the final minute.

I was a graduate student at Miami (Ohio) at the time, and I was fascinated by the decision and the uproar it created.

This game featured the Jets' Joe Namath and the Raiders' Daryle Lamonica as the two quarterbacks. Both teams were 7–2 and had their eyes on a Super Bowl berth.

No thought was put into the idea that this game might last too long. Back then, there was no overtime for regular season games. Ties were allowed, and games usually didn't last three hours.

The original schedule did show the game starting at 4:00 PM ET and then the entertainment division taking over the network at 7:00 for the showing of the made-for-TV movie *Heidi*, starring Jennifer Edwards, Maximilian Schell, Jean Simmons, and Michael Redgrave.

This was an important movie because Timex had purchased each of the advertising time slots. This was supposed to be a lucrative night for NBC.

But network executives were watching the game and concluded the game should be shown in its entirety. They were on top of it, realizing that a short delay to *Heidi* was the best solution. The new plan: the game would stay on and *Heidi* would start at its conclusion.

The NBC executives tried to convey that to the 30 Rockefeller Plaza studio but couldn't push through the switchboard, which was being besieged by callers wanting to know if *Heidi* would start on time or demanding that the football game stay on.

Not hearing any orders to the contrary, the control room operator followed the original plan and dutifully switched to the family movie exactly at 7:00.

At the time, the Jets led 32–29 with 1:05 remaining in the game.

What followed was an explosion of irate fans jamming the NBC switchboard to express displeasure. What made the situation worse for NBC was that the Raiders rallied to score two touchdowns and won 43–32. No one east of Denver was able to see that.

The next day, the "*Heidi* game" fiasco was a national story.

According to old news accounts, on the NBC Nightly News, with Chet Huntley and David Brinkley, the next day, Brinkley reported: "Fans who missed it could not be consoled."

This was long before we could use our phones to get a minute-by-minute update. We didn't have ESPN giving us a complete sports report every night at 11:00 PM. Many people didn't even know the Raiders won until they read it in the newspaper the next day. Huntley and Brinkley did show the final 1:05 on their program.

Legend has it that some people paid off bets because they believed the Jets had won that game.

NBC was pilloried for the better part of 24 hours. The events changed television. A "*Heidi* phone" was installed in every studio so executives could bypass the switchboard to get through with urgency when it was needed.

The fan reaction also made it clear how popular football had become in America.

What I saw from my perspective as a student was fodder for a paper for my broadcasting seminar class.

I called NBC sports director Carl Lindemann to interview him about what happened. His firm, albeit polite office assistant informed me that he didn't want to talk about it, at least not to a nearsighted student in Oxford, Ohio.

The next time I thought about Lindemann was 28 years later when I was wondering whether Fox Sports was going to have its version of a *Heidi* moment.

Led by Australian-born David Hill, Fox television had jumped into sports broadcasting in a major way in 1993 by acquiring the rights to National Football League games for $1.58 billion. In 1994, Fox outbid CBS to secure NHL rights. Fox paid $155 million for five seasons of NHL rights starting in the 1994–95 season.

Fox hired me to be its lead announcer and announced an innovative plan to use what was called "Fox Trax" to enhance viewer experience. Through computer graphics, Fox put a comet tail behind slap shots, showed velocity through miles per hour, and inserted a halo around the puck to allow it to be more easily seen.

Fox Trax was a story in that first season. In an old-school league like the NHL, not everyone loves innovations.

"Rats" were another hot NHL topic for the 1995–96 season. The story began one night in the dressing room of an aging Miami Arena. The Florida Panthers had to deal with what was termed a "rat invasion."

The invasion consisted of one rat and I was told that Panthers right winger Scott Mellanby dispatched it with what was described as a "strong wrister."

159

That night, he ended up scoring two goals and John Vanbiesbrouck called it a "rat trick."

The tale of Mellanby the rat slayer spread across the land, and by the playoffs the fans were littering the ice with plastic rats each time the Panthers scored a goal.

The number of rats tossed numbered in the thousands. The delay to clean them up often seemed interminable. Workers used plastic garbage cans and snow shovels to scoop them off the ice. The scene often looked hilarious as custodial employees, wearing skates, worked ankle- or knee-deep in plastic rats trying to shovel them up before more came cascading from the stands.

Our Fox cameras even caught Marti Huizenga, the wife of Panthers owner Wayne Huizenga, carrying a grocery store bag full of rats to her seat.

Opponents complained. Safety issue. Game disruption. Penguins goalie Tom Barrasso hid in his net one night after yielding a goal to the home team.

The cleanups of the rats often took 10 minutes or longer, meaning games took longer to complete. That was a concern for people, but playoff games always have the potential to run long because of overtime.

There was no worry about a rat delay on May 12, 1996, because the game was in Philadelphia. Fox scheduled the second-round playoff game between the Panthers and Philadelphia Flyers at 3:00 PM. At 7:00, Fox was supposed to show the fresh-from-the-theaters movie *Mrs. Doubtfire*, starring Robin Williams.

Fox had shelled out a considerable sum for the right to show this movie.

Is this story starting to sound familiar?

I knew nothing about the *Mrs. Doubtfire* issue. The morning production meeting was standard operating procedure. In theory, we should not have had a problem. We slotted three hours for a game. Even if it went into overtime, we still thought we'd be fine.

But before the meeting ended, producer Richie Zyontz told me it would not be fine if we had a lengthy overtime.

"Doc," he said. "If we go to a second overtime, and it gets close to 7:00, you will have a card to read. And I'm sure you won't like it."

He was correct. I didn't like it.

The card read something like this: "For those of you in the Mountain and Pacific time zones, we continue our coverage of the Stanley Cup Playoffs. For those of you in the Eastern and Central time zones, we send you to the feature film *Mrs. Doubtfire*, starring Robin Williams."

Thanks to acrobatic goaltending by Florida's John Vanbiesbrouck and Philadelphia's Ron Hextall, the game did slide into overtime. Just our luck, it was still 1–1 after the first OT period.

The clock was racing toward 7:00. I was envisioning the furor that would be created by the decision to embrace *Mrs. Doubtfire*. My partner John Davidson and I always had to defend the "glowing puck." Now the question was going to be: is Fox truly committed to hockey?

But at 6:54, Richie whispered into my headset, "Doc, you won't have to read the card."

Afterward, the rumor was that Hill had phoned Fox majority owner Rupert Mudoch to gain permission to delay the movie. Hill was a hilarious, entertaining fellow. I'm not surprised he would be able to talk Murdoch into changing the plans.

The movie wasn't delayed long. At 7:12, Panthers winger Mike Hough scored from the left circle. We showed one replay. Over the celebration shot, I added, "Rats are flying all across living rooms in south Florida."

In less than a minute, we saw the Fox monolith. Then the movie started.

161

The Year of the Rats was fun in 1995–96. But the NHL decided it was too much of a good thing. According to NHL Rule 63.4, "When objects are thrown on the ice during a stoppage in play, including after the scoring of a goal, the Referee shall have announced over the public address system that any further occurrences will result in a bench minor penalty being assessed to the home team."

That ended rat-throwing celebrations, although in 2016 the Panthers were penalized twice because fans wouldn't stop throwing plastic rats. Apparently, some still miss that tradition.

Truth is, I had a good time at Fox. The technology made it fun and I didn't mind defending the glowing puck on radio shows. We had some quality playoffs, although we had too many sweeps. At the time, we also had a shared arrangement with ESPN, resulting in a shared Stanley Cup Final. Some years we got one game of the Final and other years we had two. That was frustrating.

In 1998, ABC outbid Fox and others for the NHL's TV rights by offering $600 million over five years. I ended up as one of three play-by-play broadcasters as ABC regionalized three games at once around the country.

If you look at my résumé, you would see that I've worked for ESPN, ABC, CBS, Fox, Lifetime, SportsChannel, MSG, and finally NBC.

The real story of this book may be that I can't hold a job.

HEARTBREAK

When Columbus Blue Jackets coach John Tortorella announced in 2017 that he would miss the NHL All-Star Game to take care of his son's ailing 10-year-old pit bull, Emma, no one respected and supported his decision more than I did.

In 2002, I chose not to broadcast the Winter Olympic Games for NBC in Salt Lake City because our Yorkshire terrier was seriously ill.

Not everyone appreciated the decisions Tortorella and I made regarding our animals.

When NBC announced my situation, one columnist crudely wrote, "Some guys would run over their dog to do an Olympics."

But most pet owners understood. Our animals give us affection, unwavering loyalty, and hours of joy, and, in return, we are obligated to do all that we can to take care of them. Our pets become members of our family, and we treat them as such.

Tortorella's story had an extra layer of sentimentality because his son, Nick, Emma's master, was a U.S. Army Ranger stationed overseas. Tortorella was looking after Nick's dog while he was serving his country. To me, it seemed like a noble decision to render aid and comfort to Emma when Nick couldn't.

My dog tale started in 1998 when Joyce accompanied me on a New Jersey Devils road trip to south Florida to play the Panthers. Having only just returned from the Olympics in Nagano, I was having difficulty staying awake during the dinner hour.

We were dining at a restaurant in Miami's South Beach. It was only 7:30. But I was half asleep as our food was being served. My body was on Japanese time, which was 13 hours ahead of Miami. My clock was upside down.

Joyce took pity on me and said: "We should go back to the hotel." I agreed.

A row of taxis stood at the ready when we ventured outside. Joyce chose the one with a cute little dog sitting on the roof of the car.

As soon as we settled into the backseat, the driver plopped his tiny Yorkshire terrier named Bebe on Joyce's lap. The dog sat calmly and gazed into Joyce's eyes. It was love at first sight. It was as if we knew instantly our lives were going to change. We probably knew that night that we were going to become a dog family.

The Devils were not playing the Panthers until the following night at Miami Arena. This was the last season the Panthers played there before moving to a new building in Sunrise. Joyce had planned a day of shopping at Sawgrass Mills, an outlet mall located a lengthy distance from our hotel. She hired Bebe and the driver to take her there.

She was just as fascinated with Bebe as we were the night before.

"You know, Peter Falk rode in this car once," the driver told us, "and he offered me a thousand dollars for her."

We understood Falk's preoccupation with this petite dog. She had a charm that was difficult to describe.

When we returned home to Michigan, we took stock of our lives and realized we had no reason not to adopt a dog. Our condo association permitted dogs, provided they weighed less than 20 pounds.

Our search for a dog began. It didn't take long.

One of Joyce's co-workers raised Yorkies and was hooked up with several friends who also bred them.

The next spring, a little baby Yorkshire named Katie Joy came into our lives.

Yorkies, by their terrier nature, are chewers, pullers, and chasers, and what they lack in size they make up for in personality. Once when I was on the phone with Joyce, she began laughing uncontrollably. She said Katie was dragging a newspaper across the floor to amuse herself. Paper training turned out not to be a snap. But the loving bond between Joyce and Katie came quickly. Small dog. Big bed. It took Katie a day to secure a place in the bed.

At that time in our lives, we spent two months at a summer cottage in northern lower Michigan, in Petoskey. Guaranteed five walks a day. Katie loved the place.

During the season, Katie kept Joyce company when I was on the road. It was even more fun when the three of us were together. She loved to ride in the car. She would sleep in a small cushioned laundry basket. We had routines. If Joyce was grocery shopping, I would wait in the car and pop in what we called "Katie's CD." These were bedtime songs created to put children to sleep. But they worked on Katie as well.

Just after Christmas in 2001, we took Katie to the veterinarian for a routine checkup. That was right before I left on a road trip to Vancouver. During a layover in Toronto, I received a distressing call from Joyce. Katie's bloodwork showed kidney values well beyond the normal range. Kidney disease was feared.

"She's not even three years old," I said, shocked at the news. "How can she be that bad already?"

After landing in Vancouver, I called the veterinarian, who recommended a special diet for a month to see if her kidney numbers would change. We didn't know anything about canine kidney functions, but we had faith in our veterinarian. We opted to follow his plan. But after a short time, there wasn't much progress and we knew drastic measures might be required to save our little girl. The Internet told us there wasn't much that could be done.

Looking for kidney experts, we took Katie to a respected clinic in the Detroit area. Initially, they were optimistic. But quickly they began to talk in terms of euthanizing Katie.

"She is not even three!" I muttered those words to myself several times.

Joyce and I agonized day and night. We were not prepared to end Katie's life. She was hospitalized and we could visit her a couple of times a day. With the understanding and agreement of MSG and Devils general manager Lou Lamoriello personally, I was missing Devils games as we sorted out our options. Decisions had to be made. The 2002 Olympics in Salt Lake City were about 10 days away. It was clear to me that I wouldn't be helping anyone by going to the Olympics. I wasn't going to leave Joyce alone to deal with Katie's terminal illness. And if I was being honest with myself, I would not have been at my best for NBC had I fulfilled my duties as a broadcaster.

Because my bosses at Madison Square Garden Television had been so accommodating to give me time off from Devils broadcasts, I hoped NBC would be the same. This was not an easy ask. The Olympics are a major event on NBC's calendar. But my agent, Dennis Holland, called and explained my situation. The bottom line: I wasn't mentally prepared to be 1,769 miles from home.

NBC officials were disappointed, but sympathetic. Fortunately, talented Kenny Albert was available to step in for every game.

Although the one columnist's criticism of my decision was brought to our attention, Joyce and I weren't searching the newspaper to gauge media reaction. We can only guess that there were others who didn't understand my decision.

All I cared about was that I had the time to devote to Katie's care. The Internet in 2002 wasn't as mature as it is today, but I spent hours upon hours researching information about kidney disease and kidney transplants for dogs. A kidney transplant seemed like our only option. My research showed that kidney transplantation in dogs was dangerous, but I also discovered a 24/7 clinic at the University of California at Davis that specialized in the procedure.

I called the clinic, and then I contacted our accountant, Dale Lasharook, and asked him for a recommendation for cashing out one of our investments. He was a hunting dog owner, and he fully understood and supported our decision.

The money was spent to charter a private jet to transport Katie to the California clinic. Given the gravity of her illness, we didn't believe she could survive the trauma of a cross-country flight on a commercial airliner.

At 4:30 PM ET, we checked out of a Detroit animal hospital. That night, at 2:00 AM Pacific time, Katie was being examined and admitted at the University of California facility. Dr. Liberty Rasor oversaw her care. The veterinarians believed Katie was a viable candidate for a transplant.

The way the animal transplantation program worked was, you arrive with one dog and go home with two. You must agree to adopt the donor dog. Joyce's stepfather had already agreed to take care of the donor dog. We were given a tour of the facility where the donor dogs were cared for.

For three days, optimism reigned. We had no concern when a veterinarian came to take Katie for routine tests. We had been playing with Katie on a blanket right before a doctor had carried her away.

My phone rang a half hour later.

"This is not good news," the doctor said.

Katie had suffered a seizure while being tested. She had received immediate emergency care, but lost oxygen to the brain. She had to be placed on a respirator. Because the respirator is so unnatural for an animal, she had to be heavily sedated. She was not going to recover.

It took us a full day to accept the devastating prognosis. It was a shock. We were given hope and then the hope was stripped away by an unforeseen complication.

When it was time to say good-bye, I held Katie's paw and whispered to her repeatedly what a good dog she was. I told her that my mom, who she had met at a nursing home, would take care of her in heaven. I kept this stream of talk going until two doctors, tending to her, told me she was gone. Then, all of us cried.

No rules are in place to tell you how soon—if at all—you should adopt another dog. We began the search within a week of returning from California. It's not that we weren't grieving over Katie's loss; the memories of her remain in our hearts even today. But the sadness was overwhelming. We returned to Michigan to a home that was all about her toys, treats, dishes, blankets...

We felt an emptiness and a desire to love another dog. We needed another dog to help us mourn.

We soon located another Yorkie. We named her Liberty to honor the doctor who had tried to save Katie.

Edward Grinnan is a dog lover, a Detroit Red Wings fan, and the editor of *Guideposts* magazine—a faith-based publication founded by minister and author Norman Vincent Peale. Shortly after the time came for one of his dogs to leave this earth, he wrote:

"Where does the dog go? I think heaven. If you are a doubter that animals go to heaven, I feel sorry for you. Either animals go there or no one goes there, because I cannot imagine a God who could contrive paradise without animals and the love and joy they bring us. What kind of a cruel heaven would that be? The fact that we can share the deepest and most complex emotions with our pets is proof. Only through the alchemy of two souls meeting can this kind of love take hold. And a soul lives beyond its own mantle. A soul belongs in heaven."

Fellow broadcaster Bryant Gumbel had owned a Yorkshire terrier and he sent me a thoughtful condolence note after Katie's death. It was one of about 80 letters we received after it was announced why I missed the Olympics.

Paul Harvey Jr., son of the famed broadcaster, was among those who reached out to us to offer support. I had long been a listener to his father's broadcasts.

After I returned to work on Devils broadcasts, veteran New Jersey center Bobby Holik gave me a wrapped gift. It was a book called *Dog Heaven* by Cynthia Rylant. It's a soulful, comforting book for those who have recently lost a dog.

Rylant penned beautiful words about dogs eating "ham-sandwich biscuits" and "sleeping on cloud beds" in heaven. She helps you smile through your grief.

Joyce and I were touched by the thoughtfulness of the Holiks' gift. You don't expect to receive a gift from a player. That's not the nature of a relationship between a broadcaster and athlete. But Bobby and Renee Holik raise horses. Their daughter, Hannah, was an accomplished equestrian competitor. They understood how attached a person can become to an animal. They empathized with the grief we were experiencing. We appreciated their help.

In our house today, in a corner where our dogs' water and food bowls are located, we have photos of our dogs past and present. The *Dog Heaven* book stands there in a place of prominence.

Our love of animals has only increased over time. Today, we have two Yorkshire Terriers named Joy Bells and Liberty II. We've also spread our animal love to other varieties.

YOU WOULD THINK AFTER DECADES together, I would know everything there is to know about Joyce. But in 2004 I discovered that wasn't true. During the 2004–05 lockout, when the entire NHL season was canceled, I discovered my wife had dreamed of owning a horse since she was a little girl.

Twins generally know every detail about each other, but even Joyce's twin, Bob, didn't know she longed for a horse during her childhood.

They grew up in a normal-sized two-bedroom home built by her father in Port Huron, located on a normal-sized lot. The family made room for cats, dogs, even a monkey. But their property could not have accommodated a horse.

What became clear is that Joyce was interested in owning one and, with simple investigation, we discovered available horses are plentiful. And there are an ample number of barns and stables to rent for a horse.

Through a "friend of a friend" we got our horse in time for Christmas. His formal name is Rey San Lynx. His barn name is Dino. He was six when we acquired him. He had been a competition cutting horse. Cutting is a Western-style equine competition in which a horse and rider work together to show the horse's athleticism and ability to handle cattle. Out west, it's a job. Working horses are highly valued.

The plan was for Joyce to learn to ride Dino, although he had other plans. Horses can live beyond age 30, meaning Dino was still relatively young. He wasn't calm enough to be ridden by a beginner.

Right after Dino joined us, we made a trip to the county fairgrounds and discovered a sad-looking white Arabian horse who had been left in a field to starve to death. A kind woman named Pat had taken her in, nursed her back to health, and was looking for someone to adopt her for the price of her veterinarian bills. Those totaled $240.

Then the Emrick stable had two horses.

Sassy Pants, as we called her, would never be ridden. Our plan was just to give her a quality life. We believe she is 31 today, although we really don't know for sure.

Still looking for a riding horse for Joyce, we purchased a 17-year-old retired cutting horse named Proclaim My Fame. We discovered him giving rides to children. He was a perfect horse for Joyce.

But we still weren't done. We brought in Pooh Bear. She was big, beautiful, and the fourth horse in our stable. Her father was a champion in the reigning tradition. His name was Done It Out West. Pooh Bear was also a reigning horse but did not compete that way. For us she was a pet. But she finished in the top five in the state of Michigan twice as a show horse. For amateurs like myself, those competitions are like beauty contests, without the swimsuit competition. Lots of thorough washing, black paint on hooves, etc.

We still were not finished adopting horses. The *Port Huron Times Herald* published a story, with a darling photograph, about a mini-horse named Prancer who was the last animal remaining from a local shelter that was closing. These are animals you might see in a circus. Prancer is the size of a Great Dane. Prancer was living on table scraps. Horses don't do well by themselves. They need company. We couldn't leave the horse by himself. Within two days, the adoption processed, and Prancer was ours.

It never surprises me when Joyce steps up to take care of animals. I've seen it often. Once, when Joyce heard that local animal control had rescued 20 cats from a hoarder, she and a friend drove to see the veterinarian who was taking care of the animals. They were all being spayed and neutered. Figuring that animal control would be hard-pressed to fit that cost into its budget, Joyce paid the entire veterinarian bill.

We seem to be holding steady at five horses now, although some may say we have four and a half, based on Prancer's size. Joyce's brother and I shake our heads over the size of the Emrick stable. Neither of us saw this coming. Joyce dearly loves these 1,200-pound creatures.

What I've learned about horses is that these beautiful animals eat much more than Yorkshire Terriers.

MADCAP COACHES AND
A CAMEL AT THE DOOR

The late minor league coach Terry Slater once boasted to reporters he could prove International Hockey League referees were incompetent by running across the ice during a game without officials seeing him.

One night in the 1960s, while coaching the Toledo Blades against the Port Huron Flags, he made good on that promise.

I met many colorful characters in my seven-year minor league broadcasting career, but none more fascinating than Slater, who I met before I worked in the IHL.

My first encounter with Slater came during the 1968–69 season, before I landed my first play-by-play job, while I was a master's degree aspirant at Miami (Ohio). As part of an independent study program, I conducted radio interviews in every IHL city except Des Moines because I couldn't afford to travel there. The purpose was to create a four-part, two-hour documentary-like story about life in the IHL. You could say Slater was one of the stars of the production, or least one of the more compelling interview subjects.

The question-and-answer session I conducted with Slater, where I learned the details of his mad dash across the ice, was included in one of the four half-hour IHL radio segments that aired on the Miami University radio station.

By the time I was in the Miami postgraduate programs, my sights had long been set on broadcasting in the IHL. But my tour of the IHL, which included interviews with madcap personalities like Slater and an assortment of other coaches, players, and general managers, reaffirmed my belief that I needed to work in this world of lengthy bus rides, line brawls, and zany promotional ideas.

It was Slater who didn't quite seem to belong there. On paper, he was the last guy you would expect to make a farce out of a hockey game. He was a St. Lawrence University graduate with an erudite approach to life. But like every IHL coach, he also wanted to win, and he believed inconsistent officiating sometimes prevented him from doing that. He also understood that one of his duties as a minor league coach was selling the game. That's why he would occasionally transform a game into theater of the absurd.

The first time I laid eyes on Slater was at the Toledo Sports Arena, where I found him in the box office taking ticket reservations over the telephone.

As he hung up the receiver, I heard him say: "It's going to be a madhouse in here tomorrow."

Slater was an effective coach—he won the IHL championship in his first season with the Blades in 1966–67. He was also a showman. He understood he needed to be another P.T. Barnum to coax fans into the less-than-glamourous Toledo Sports Arena. He had pieced together a roster of veteran players like Stan "Chook" Maxwell and William "Chick" Chalmers. He didn't have a bunch of younger players who would have rushed into the seats fighting for him. He had to discover creative ways to fill his building.

When you couple that line of thinking with Slater's belief that IHL officiating was inferior, you end up with the crazy night Slater sprinted through the neutral zone. I still possess the tape of my interview with Slater when he explained why he pulled off that stunt.

Bill Doyle was the referee, and he didn't spot Slater, dressed in suit and tie, zipping across center ice. Bob McCammon was playing center for the Flags, and when I talked to him about the story several years later, he recalled being the one who brought Slater's antics to Doyle's attention.

"Did you see what Slater just did?" a stunned McCammon asked Doyle.

"Son," Doyle said, "don't get your shorts in a knot. I'm going to find out."

Slater told me that he denied he had been on the ice. "I'm the general manager," Slater told Doyle. "Geez, the score was 5–0 and the game was over as far as I was concerned. I just walked around the rink."

Doyle undoubtedly was miffed to find Slater sitting smugly in the penalty box. We can guess that every IHL referee had heard of Slater's pledge, reported thoroughly by newspapers, to protest officiating in this fashion. At the very least, referees understood that he didn't think much of their work. He was never shy about voicing that opinion.

Slater was assessed a two-minute bench penalty and was ejected from the game. Doyle said those penalties were going to be the least of Slater's problems. He told Slater he would be fined "and a lot is going to happen from this." Slater recalled the fine was $500 and he didn't believe he ever paid it. He was also suspended two games. But even if he had paid the fine, Slater said it would have been worth it to demonstrate to officials what was happening around them. He believed referees were missing way too many penalties and linesmen were not even on top of icing calls.

"I made a mockery of the game, but I proved a point," Slater told me.

In six seasons as an IHL coach, Slater received more than his fair share of stern telephone calls from the commissioner about his antics.

One day in Toledo, he informed members of the media that the team had signed a new player with "a very suspicious background."

Slater would not say who the player was, nor was a press release issued, because he didn't want the IHL office to know his plans before the player participated in his first game.

That night, a player wearing a pro wrestling mask participated in the warm-ups. The mystery player turned out to be Slater, who had been an exceptional college player at St. Lawrence. As a 145-pound center, Slater averaged better than two points per game (75 goals and 167 points in 76 games) in three seasons for the Saints. He had played three minor league seasons before diving into the coaching profession.

Slater was skilled at using the media to sell tickets for him. He always tried to feed reporters a story that created the kind of headlines that would spike ticket sales. But Slater never schemed without a specific objective in mind.

The Des Moines Oak Leafs liked to play home games on Friday and Saturday nights. Much to Slater's dismay, the IHL would sometimes also schedule the Oak Leafs to play Sunday afternoon at 3:00 PM on the road after those Friday-Saturday home games.

To understand the consternation that caused for the Oak Leafs, consider that the Fort Wayne Komets were the closest opponent to Des Moines. That trip from Des Moines to Fort Wayne was 479 miles, a bus trip of more than eight hours. Slater believed that three games in two and a half days, with a draining bus ride in the mix, was a major disadvantage for his team.

That's why Slater was sure that the Dayton Gems insisted he needed to play a 3:00 PM game on a Sunday in Dayton against the Oak Leafs. It was a 579-mile all-night drive for Slater's team after playing on back-to-back nights.

As the bus was pulling into Dayton on that Sunday, Slater told his bus driver that he needed to stop at Kmart before completing the trip to the arena.

He entered the store and came out with bags full of nightshirts, the long, flowing pajama shirts that you would see in a presentation of Charles Dickens' *A Christmas Carol.*

When the Oak Leafs stepped on the ice for warm-ups in Dayton, they were all wearing nightshirts. Slater had made his point and Dayton fans had a few laughs.

Revenge was on Slater's mind when he once planted microphones in the visiting dressing room before a game against Dayton. He made it obvious they were there. He wanted microphones discovered because he wanted the Gems to believe he was spying on them.

Slater's secret was that the microphones were not connected to any device that allowed them to transmit. They were inoperable. They were just for show.

He parked outside the visiting dressing room between periods, and didn't hear a sound coming out of the room. The Gems sat in silence because they believed the Des Moines coach was listening.

The fact that Dayton coaches and players weren't discussing what was happening on the ice was even better than Slater actually knowing what their plans were. He had successfully disrupted the Gems' communication.

What Slater remembered most about the incident was that the Oak Leafs had won the game. The IHL investigated, but Slater was able to prove that he installed a bunch a "dead wires" with no purpose other than to "psyche out" his opponents. In his mind, his team's victory showed his plan had succeeded.

Slater found success after he left the IHL. He coached in the now-defunct World Hockey Association with the Los Angeles Sharks (1972–74) and Cincinnati Stingers (1975–77). He then moved to the college ranks to coach at Colgate starting in 1978–79.

He held that post for 14 years before dying from a stroke on his 54th birthday in 1991. Two seasons before, Colgate had made a memorable run to the NCAA championship game only to lose to Wisconsin.

ANOTHER UNFORGETTABLE CHARACTER FROM MY tenure in the IHL was coach Ted Garvin. Because Garvin spent five seasons coaching the Port Huron Flags, it's presumed we connected there in the 1970s. But after Garvin took the Flags to the Turner Cup Final in 1972–73, he was hired to coach the NHL's Detroit Red Wings. My arrival in Port Huron came weeks after his departure.

But Garvin was fired by the Red Wings after 11 games, and he was back in the IHL coaching the Toledo Goaldiggers to a Turner Cup championship.

Like Slater, Garvin could be as entertaining as he was effective at his job. His preferred method of protesting officiating calls was to throw towels into the crowd. One night in Fort Wayne, Garvin hurled so many towels into the stands that Komets management sent him a bill for missing towels. Fort Wayne fans took them home as souvenirs.

Garvin's response was to send a package of paper towels to management. He offered his hope that his towels would adequately replace the lost Komet towels.

It was Garvin's nature to be dramatic, especially before a faceoff. That was the time he liked to make a statement about what he thought of the officiating or the way the game was going.

One night, he was trailing 5–0 against the Flags, and he sent out his tough guy line of Willie Trognitz, Doug Mahood, and Paul Tantardini. He then made a public display of calling those players back to the bench for another conference as if they didn't know what was expected of them.

When the referee got everyone back on the ice, the puck was dropped and the gloves were immediately dropped as well.

That's the way the game was played back in the 1970s. The Boston Bruins and Philadelphia Flyers were winning with tough teams and that strategy was also selling tickets in the minor leagues.

The Toledo Blades weren't drawing well in the IHL, and that team was moved to Lansing, Michigan, where it didn't last a full season.

Former IHL commissioner Andy Mulligan had started hockey anew in Toledo with the introduction of the Toledo Goaldiggers. Garvin was brought back to wave towels, stir up fans, and create a winning product.

Garvin's theatrics, an emphasis on fighting, and 10-cent beer nights helped boost attendance for the new-look Toledo team. The Goaldiggers weren't bringing in the family crowd they would later draw, but they were attracting a crowd.

Garvin knew how to fill the stands. At one point, the Goaldiggers were struggling on the ice, and insightful *Toledo Blade* columnist John Gugger penned a column saying Garvin was doing all he could to turn the team around.

The headline: "Garvin Is Not Superman."

That night Garvin came out behind the bench wearing a cape, with a yellow shirt adorned with a giant "S" on the front.

In 1974–75, Garvin's Goaldiggers finished with a 34–38–4 record and then won the IHL playoff championship. Maybe Garvin was Superman.

ALTHOUGH MOST OF MY 45-YEAR pro hockey career has been spent in the NHL, I enjoyed my days in the minors just as much as I have those in the NHL. The people I met in the early days of my career are as important as the NHL folks I know today.

Archie Henderson played for the Port Huron Flags, after I had left to join the Maine Mariners. But he was one of Morris Snider's favorite players. He was one of the minor league's toughest fighters, but that's not why Snider like him.

Archie was as lovable as they come, a man who stood 6-foot-6 and owned a kind heart and a caring personality. When Henderson fought, he was merely playing a role, like an actor in a stage performance. That's not who he was as a person.

A sentimental man, Henderson called Snider crying after he played his first NHL game with the Washington Capitals in 1980–81.

"I just wanted to know what it was like to stand there for the anthem as an NHL player, and now I know," Henderson said.

As I got to know Henderson through the years, I viewed him as more evidence that tough guys were some of the warmest-hearted guys pro hockey has ever produced.

His statistics show that he played 23 NHL games and amassed 92 penalty minutes. He had a ferocious side, but mostly he was funny and emotional.

In 1983–84, Henderson was playing for coach Nick Beverley on the New Haven Nighthawks. With one game left in the season, Henderson informed reporters that he was leaning toward retiring at the end of the season. He was 19 minutes short of 2,000 minor league penalty minutes and his plan was to pick up those final 19 minutes in the last game at Hershey and then call it a career.

Hershey players had all read the newspapers, as had referee Bill McCreary, who was assigned to that game. Everyone knew what was coming. It was hardly a surprise when Henderson put a beating on Hershey defenseman Jim Burton.

"What do I get?" Henderson asked McCreary as he headed to the penalty box.

"Two, five, and a game misconduct—you are two minutes short, have a nice summer," McCreary supposedly said.

At an NHL game years later, I ran into McCreary after a game and asked him to confirm the details. He said he remembered "something like that" but came up short when it came to providing a full confirmation.

The funny element of the story is that Henderson opted not to retire after the season. He played four more seasons and added 920 more penalty minutes.

My favorite Henderson story came after he retired, when I was interviewing him for a Port Huron early morning radio show.

Because he was living in Calgary, in the Mountain time zone, I suggested we tape an interview so he didn't have to get up before dawn to talk to me on my morning show. He suggested that I ask him about the legendary episode involving Henderson stealing the Toledo Goaldiggers pregame pucks before warm-ups.

According to the legend, Henderson told Toledo players they would have to fight him to get their pucks returned.

Per his suggestion, I teed it up for him on the radio interview, noting that younger Port Huron listeners may not have heard about the night he held a bucket of pucks hostage.

"I'm glad you asked me about that, Mike, because that story has dogged me for my entire career, and it makes me mad because the story is false," he said.

He paused for effect, then said: "It was actually against Saginaw."

It was impossible not to enjoy time spent with Henderson. One of the fondest memories of Henderson is the story of his last visit to Port Huron's McMorran Arena. Henderson only played the 1977–78 season in Port Huron, but Snider always considered him one of the franchise's most memorable players. They kept in contact, and one season Henderson came back to the arena and he and Snider stood on the bridge behind the net that connected both sides of the stands. No seats were located behind the net at McMorran.

When it was time for Henderson to leave, he asked Snider if he would join him for a word of prayer. Morris said it was a nice prayer, and he was touched by the gesture.

My feeling was Henderson knew he would probably never see Snider again and he wanted to share a final moment with him. That's the kind of man Henderson is. He appreciated Snider as much as I did.

Morris was special. I had heard about Snider before I had met him.

During my Miami University independent study program on the IHL, I drove my Volkswagen Beetle from Oxford, Ohio, to Dayton as often I could to watch the Gems as a reporter for the 1968–69 season.

My treasured press pass earned me a seat next to *Dayton Daily News* beat writer D.L. Stewart, who filled my brain with useful and fun information about the IHL. I was a sponge, soaking up whatever would spill out of Stewart.

I also met Edgar "Lefty" McFadden, the genial Gems general manager who would later become one of my frequent pregame and between-period interview guests. The interesting element of McFadden's career was that he never played a game of hockey but rose to become a highly respected general manager.

McFadden was another IHL executive who understood the art of promoting his sport. He placed girls with pom-poms at every entrance and brought in high school bands to keep his fans entertained.

The other person I got to know in Dayton was Gems broadcaster Lyle Stieg, who had previously been a broadcaster in Port Huron.

That turned out to be an important detail four years later when I interviewed with Wismer for the Flags broadcast job. One of my first calls went to Stieg to find out about Wismer and the Flags.

"You're going to love Port Huron," Stieg said. "The players taught me the game. I didn't know a faceoff from a bale of hay when I came to Port

Huron. I learned from guys like your new coach Bobby McCammon. And John Wismer will treat you right."

McFadden was equally laudatory of the Flags organization.

"Get down to the arena and see Morris Snider right away. A prince of a guy. I mean it—a prince," McFadden said.

Both assessments were on the mark.

In my seven years of broadcasting in the IHL and AHL, no one taught me as much about the game as McCammon, who went on to coach in the NHL with the Philadelphia Flyers (1978–79, 1981–84) and Vancouver Canucks (1987–1991).

At the precise moment I was walking by the famed McMorran Tower, McCammon was unlocking the door to his office, which was located between the two rinks. He immediately invited me to lunch and our friendship was born. It continues to this day.

All of the Fort Wayne players that I idolized were McCammon's contemporaries, and he had opinions and tales about all of them. He kept me entertained with stories and insights. He had me laughing for the entire lunch with his humorous takes about hockey life.

He gave me a player's perspective and the inside scoop on a pregame brawl that had occurred the previous spring, when the Komets and Flags had met in the playoffs.

"It was a free-for-all," McCammon said. "Skeets Harrison was the referee but it wasn't his job to watch the warm-up. After he heard what was going on, he walked on the ice with a Styrofoam cup of coffee in one hand and a cigar in the other trying to get everybody to settle down."

At my first lunch with McCammon, he also told me that I wasn't going to find a better boss than Flags general manager Morris Snider.

"He's had a lot of high-pressure jobs, so he keeps a case of 12 bottles of Maalox behind his desk," McCammon said. "Occasionally, you will see him reach down and take a swig."

But above all, McCammon insisted, Snider "just wants to be your friend."

He was right. As much as McCammon taught me about the game, Snider taught me about balancing my hockey life. He worked hard, but found time for other pursuits.

Earning $160 per week, I was always counting my nickels and dimes. When I dined at Saffee's restaurant, I'd often just order a baked potato. I could save on calories as well as money. At least, that's what I told myself.

But when Snider was in the restaurant at the same time, he would occasionally invite me over to enjoy a steak on his tab.

After my first season as Flags broadcaster and WHLS sports director, Snider asked me to become a half-time public relations director for the Flags. At that point, I found myself with two half-time jobs totaling more than 80 hours per week in the winter. Snider paid more than half of my salary. Radio station raises were not nearly as large, or as frequent, as pay increases Snider gave me during my time in Port Huron. He was a mentor and friend.

He did chug Maalox like it was Coca-Cola and was a genuine miracle-worker with his smoke-and-mirrors ability to keep the Flags financially afloat.

His penny-pinching was legendary when it came to player contracts. He had to hold the line on player costs or the $300,000 per year losses would have been worse.

One of my fondest memories was the day of the Flags' first game of the 1975–76 season, when Morris ordered the bus to be started as he negotiated with a young player named Danny Newman.

Everyone else on the team had signed and were on board waiting for the three-and-a-half-hour trip to Muskegon.

Newman sat in Snider's office and listened to a tough-love sales pitch.

"I don't think you really want to play hockey," Snider told Newman. "Only eight goals scored last season, and [coach] Bobby [McCammon] gave you ice time."

Snider simplified Newman's options as only he could. "This is your contract," he said. "You either sign it and get on the bus, or don't sign it and go home."

Newman peered down at the desk to get a look at the salary amount, but Snider's left arm conveniently covered it. All Newman could see was the X where Snider wanted him to sign.

"How much do I get?" Newman asked.

"Never you mind," Snider said. "This is your fork in the road. Either you want to play hockey or you don't. If you do, the money doesn't matter. If you don't, the money doesn't matter. Sign. Or don't sign. The bus is waiting."

Newman signed and boarded the bus.

Later, Newman learned he was the second-lowest-paid player on the team. But that year, he was one of the top 10 scorers in the IHL. The following year, Morris, Bob, and I drove to Olympia Stadium in Detroit to watch Newman skate on the left wing with center Phil Esposito and right wing Kenny Hodge for the New York Rangers.

Snider was a one-of-a-kind hockey guy. Despite the pressure he had managing the arena and the Flags hockey team, he found the time to live his life as a grandfather, motorcycle rider, and practical joker. Even in his 60s, he found it exhilarating to roar down the highway on his Harley-Davidson.

The butt of Snider's practical jokes was usually Ron Saffee, owner of Saffee's restaurant, located next to McMorran Arena.

Snider once drove his motorcycle through Saffee's restaurant. When asked about it later, Snider said only: "I messed up my knuckles on one wall trying to turn the corner near the cigarette machine."

Another day, when the circus was in Port Huron, Snider forced a camel partway through Saffee's front door as Saffee fought valiantly to prevent the beast from entering the premises. I have always wondered what Port Huron Board of Health officials would have thought had they wandered by Saffee's as the camel drama was unfolding.

We lost Morris in 2011. He was 87 when he died. Former Flags players Jim Bannatyne, Lloyd Maxfield, Larry Gould, Ray Germain, Gordie Redden, and Mike McDougal served as pallbearers at his funeral. I was honored to eulogize Snider for friends and family.

I told stories, because that's what you should do when you are honoring the memory of someone who knew how to fully explore his life.

I recounted how Snider had to stand between Ernest Tubb and a young Johnny Cash who were fixing to fight over Tubb's refusal to allow Cash to sing an encore.

According to Morris, Tubb had said: "Leave 'em wanting more."

Cash responded by destroying two guitars, and had his mind made up to destroy Tubb before Snider jumped in to prevent combat.

It wasn't the only time Snider served as a peacemaker. Dayton owner Lefty McFadden and Flags owner John Wismer almost came to blows in Wismer's office at the local radio station. Snider again stepped in to prevent arguing from escalating to fisticuffs.

Then there was the time Snider convinced the owner of the Port Huron Cunningham Drug Store to open after hours to fill an emergency prescription filled for the famed entertainer Liberace. He had fallen ill while performing at Snider's McMorran Arena.

Snider's act of kindness had resulted in Liberace and Snider becoming friends. Snider stayed at Liberace's palatial mansion in Las Vegas on more than one occasion.

After Snider's funeral, some of his children, grandchildren, and great-grandchildren said they hadn't heard some of the tales I shared about my friend.

I thought of many Snider memories after he was gone, many of them about how he helped me. He did everything he could to help me further my career.

I sat in his office multiple times and listened to him tell hockey people of power on the phone that I would be a great hire. He encouraged me to apply for the Maine Mariners broadcasting job in 1977. He said he didn't want to lose me, but he respected me enough to appreciate that I had to pursue my dreams.

One piece of advice Snider gave me was to make sure I made my new employer pay me more than he was paying me.

12
WALKING WITH ERNIE

My grandparents taught me how the U.S. Postal Service was supposed to work in the 1950s. I would mail them a letter and six days later I would receive one in return.

Three days there. Three days back. Like clockwork. That's was the letter-writing timeline as far as I was concerned. When I mailed fan letters to Chicago White Sox broadcaster Bob Elson of WCFL and Chicago Cubs announcer Jack Quinlan of WGN, I started checking our mailbox for their reply on the sixth day.

I checked again on the seventh day and the eighth day and the ninth day. I didn't give up easily. I checked every day for a couple of weeks. When you are a young boy in love with baseball, you think, this is a day when I will hear from Mr. Elson and Mr. Quinlan. But Elson and Quinlan were not my grandparents.

After about a month, I received a postcard from Quinlan with a picture of him and Lou Boudreau on it. Nothing was written on the card. Never did hear back from Elson.

When you are 12 or 13, you don't grasp what life is like. You just think Elson and Quinlan sit all day at a desk, and when the mail is dumped on said desk, they answer it promptly. When that duty was done, they went to the press box and broadcast a baseball game.

But I tell this story because when I sent Detroit Tigers broadcaster Ernie Harwell a letter in 1974 asking him to be an advisor for my PhD dissertation (from Bowling Green State University), I received a letter back in six days. Three days there. Three days back. Like clockwork.

The Detroit Tigers logo was on the envelope. I still have it.

"Sure," Ernie wrote, "come to Tiger Stadium and let's talk."

When the letter exchange occurred, I had never met the man. He had no idea who I was, other than what I told him in the letter. He knew I was a young broadcaster in Port Huron who was asking his help to complete my doctorate degree. That was enough for him to say yes, because that's the kind of human being Harwell was.

Ernie was the only person I asked to be my advisor, because he seemed like a logical choice, considering I didn't personally know anyone broadcasting at the major league level.

When my request was sent to him, the Georgia-born Harwell had already been a baseball broadcaster for 31 years, including 14 with the Detroit Tigers. He was legendary in Detroit and owned a national reputation as one of the best announcers in the game. After starting his media career as a *Sporting News* correspondent at age 16, graduating from Emory University and working as a sportswriter for the *Atlanta Constitution*, Harwell landed his first broadcasting job with the Atlanta Crackers of the Southern Association in 1943 and then worked for the Brooklyn Dodgers, New York Giants, and Baltimore Orioles before coming to Detroit. His career was interrupted once in 1943 to serve his country for four years as a U.S. Marine.

Still today, Harwell has the distinction of being the only broadcaster ever traded for a player. Dodgers general manager Branch Rickey traded catcher Cliff Dapper to the Crackers in 1948 for Harwell's contract.

Harwell, then 56, was considered an authority in his sport, and I had listened to his elegant, lyrical game calls while I was at Bowling Green and again when I reached Port Huron. His 50,000-watt WJR signal covered the 82 miles from Detroit to Bowling Green rather easily.

You didn't forget Harwell's style. He said Opening Day was like Easter Sunday at church "because you will see people that you won't see the rest of the year."

Batters didn't strike out on a called third strike when Harwell was at the microphone. He would say, "They stood there like the house by the side of the road and watched that one go by," or indicate that they had been called out "for excessive window shopping."

Instead of saying, "no runs, no hits, no errors" at the end of the inning, Harwell would sometimes say "nothing across," and everyone in Detroit knew what that mean.

It wasn't always a simple strike call. Sometimes, it was: "It's a strike, umpire Ken Kaiser said so." Harwell didn't like saying "in the windup" so he often said, "He kicks and deals."

Many young people learned their Michigan geography by listening to Harwell broadcasts, because when a foul ball reached the stands he would say, "A man from Kalamazoo got that one." Sometimes the man was from Traverse City.

Some listeners, especially the young ones, thought Harwell simply knew the regulars in the stands, although most people understood he simply fictionalized where they were from.

You probably see why I believed he would be an excellent advisor on a dissertation about the history of broadcasting dating to the 1920s.

But the most important reason I reached out to him was that I heard he was a good person. Based on that, I determined he might agree to do it.

The manner in which he replied told me that I had made the right choice. It also told me that Harwell might have some principles and manners in common with my grandparents, Lee and Metta Sharp. At the very least, they shared a belief that letters should be answered promptly.

As it turned out, they had much more in common. My grandfather was a Methodist minister and Ernie was also a man of considerable religious faith.

I made several visits to Tiger Stadium to visit him, but it was the first visit that I will always remember.

During a 30-minute interview, conducted three hours before a Tigers broadcast, he provided a wide range of stories, insight, advice, and encouragement that still resonate with me almost 50 years later.

One of my questions was about how Ernie dealt with the controversy and adversity that often crops up when you are a team broadcaster. When I did the interview, it was the year after combative Billy Martin had been fired as the Tigers manager, and iron-willed Jim Campbell was the team's general manager. They often butted heads like rams on a mountaintop. Harwell had been living in that world daily.

It's never easy for the broadcaster to navigate through those situations. Artful diplomacy is the key.

"In my experience," Ernie told me, "I've learned that you have to ride the tide."

His answers were crucial to my dissertation, but what happened afterward was perhaps even more meaningful to me as a person.

We had chatted across his desk, and when we were finished, he rose and said: "Let's go down to the press room for dinner."

His office was under the stands, well down the right-field line. The press room was behind third base at field level. You couldn't see the diamond, or stands, from the press room or his office. It was about 5:00 PM, more than two hours before game time. Batting practice hadn't started. I knew because I couldn't hear any sounds of bat on ball.

But as we walked inside the lower concourse, you could see workers were already in the concession stands, preparing the food that would be consumed by fans that night.

At one small stand, an older woman was standing, turning hot dogs on a grill. She kept staring at us. That was also true of the man, standing at a small podium, setting up his stacks of scorecards and a supply of Tigers pencils. He was continually glancing at us as he rearranged his wares.

After a few seconds, I realized they were both trying to make eye contact with Ernie, hoping he might say hello to them. He did more than that.

We went to the grill first. He greeted the woman like they were old friends.

"How is it going today?" he asked.

Almost formally, like the Southern gentleman he was, Ernie used the woman's first and last name and said: "Shake hands with a friend of mine, Mike Emrick."

We had known each other for all of 30 minutes at that time.

Ernie made small talk with the woman, asked about her family. He seemed to know quite a bit about her.

Next, we went to the scorecard podium where it was more of the same. Cheerful conversation. Expressions of respect and friendship. He used both our first and last names when he introduced us.

While I'm sure it wasn't his intention, on that day, Ernie taught an aspiring young broadcaster how to live his faith while following his dream as a broadcaster.

Fred Rogers—known to his television viewers as Mr. Rogers—was also a Presbyterian minister and he once said: "A ministry doesn't have to only be through a church. We can minister to others by being compassionate and caring."

Ernie and I also bonded over our faith. He said his life had changed by attending a Billy Graham Crusade in 1961. He told me his faith was important to him. "Some people may not want to hear this, but..." he said.

I understood. My time for that came at the Lafontaine Methodist Church. I was not even 10. During a series of meetings one night, I paid attention. Afterward, I wanted to go back to meet with one of the speakers. Reverend Barker was his name. He was a quiet, polite man, but his calm and reasoned words had powerful meaning to me. My mom went with me, and both Rev. Barker and Mom talked sincerely about whether I was making my own decision.

He asked me to read a short passage from the New Testament, 1 John, and when he was convinced I understood what he had explained to me, we shook hands. That was it. My choice was made, quietly and as dignified as I could make it.

I sensed that day that Ernie understood to have the kind of ministry that Mr. Rogers was talking about. He seemed to know how to incorporate his Christianity into his work as a broadcaster without anyone realizing his effort. Ernie was a broadcaster his entire life. But he carved out time to start the baseball chapels for players who had no opportunity to go to church before Sunday games. Ernie lived his faith.

Harwell's kindness helped me complete my dissertation and defend it by 1976.

When I tell the story of Harwell's assistance, I like to point out that Harwell didn't help me because he thought I was special. He probably offered similar acts of kindness to 200 other young broadcasters through his career.

He broadcast his last game for the Tigers in 2002 at age 84. He was 92 when he died in 2010.

I always try to pay homage to those who have helped me during my career, and Ernie deserves special mention. Ernie touched my life in a memorable way.

13

ONE SWING
AT BASEBALL

HBO's *Real Sports with Bryant Gumbel* decided to profile me in 2015, and Andrea Kremer did her usual thorough job. She spent a day with me in Boston, another in Chicago, and one more at my home in St. Clair, Michigan. She sat with Joyce and visited with our dogs and horses.

It aired Thanksgiving week, on Tuesday, November 24, and it was a humbling portrayal. When the piece was finished, Kremer and show host Bryant Gumbel chatted briefly, a television version of a postscript.

"Do you think there's anything else Doc would want to do?" Bryant asked.

"He's a Pittsburgh Pirates fan and he'd like to broadcast a Pirates game," Kremer said.

As a television man, I understood that was a perfectly clean way to wrap up the piece. But I didn't think much beyond that.

The next day was the day before Thanksgiving. I was enjoying coffee at Tim Hortons when the phone rang. I was surprised someone would be calling. I noticed it was a 314 area code. I couldn't think of anyone in St. Louis who'd be calling me.

After briefly considering allowing voice mail to take care of it, I decided to answer. I was immediately glad I did.

"Doc, Bob Costas," the familiar voice said.

I knew Bob from our NBC affiliation. He worked at some outdoor NHL games and we worked together at some Olympics. Most people don't know that Costas started his professional broadcasting career at age 21 as a $30-per-game play-by-play guy for the Syracuse Blazers in the North American Hockey League in 1973–74.

"Bob," I replied. "Hi! How are you?"

"Fine," he said. "I saw the piece on *Real Sports* last night. I think I can make that bucket list item happen."

My confusion must have registered with Costas because he immediately explained what he was talking about.

"That Pirates game," he said. "Here's what we'll do. Early next year, when our MLB Network telecast schedule comes out, we'll pick a game with the Pirates, probably in Pittsburgh on a Friday night. We'll do the game together and I'll get it started and get you to some of the Pirates you know when they're at bat and you just take it and go as long as you want. We will set this up for you to shine. One other thing—all of MLB Network's policies of impartiality will be waived in your case for that one night."

The last part was designed to make me laugh. It worked.

Obviously, this was another dream come true for me. As previously mentioned, as a child, I had wanted to be a baseball broadcaster before I wanted to be a hockey play-by-play broadcaster.

Costas got the game set up for July 8, 2016, and the Pirates were playing the Cubs that night. What made it even more special for me was that the first time I saw my team play live was against the Cubs at Wrigley Field in 1959.

To understand how important the Pirates are to me, consider that I still remember that my biology teacher, Verl Woodring, an otherwise good guy and coach of our seventh-grade basketball team, decided not to allow us to listen to the Game 7 of the 1960 World Series in his class. I'm still disappointed in that decision. That series featured the New York Yankees and my beloved Pirates.

You may have forgotten that all World Series games, until 1971, were played in the afternoon. Other teachers were kind enough to allow students to listen. But Mr. Woodring, per his right, decided we were too far behind in the study of amoeba and protozoa.

The biology room was adjacent to the study hall where students were listening to the game. Partway through my class, I detected cheering. But I didn't know if it was Yankees haters or Yankees lovers doing the cheering.

I need to frame it in those terms because there were no other Pirates fans in my section of Indiana.

It wasn't until the dismissal bell rang at 3:21 PM Central time that I discovered the wonderful news that Pirates second baseman Bill Mazeroski had delivered his monumental World Series–winning home run in the bottom of the ninth inning. Sixty years later, it's still considered among the most famous moments in World Series history.

Before that game, the only MLB experience I had was a couple of innings of a Pirates spring training game with Greg Brown and John Wehner at McKechnie Field in Bradenton, Florida. Prior to that I had not done play-by-play of a baseball game since I was a graduate student at Miami (Ohio) in 1969.

At the last minute, the campus station told me and Stan Savran to set up and broadcast the Miami–Kent State game. Savran, a longtime television broadcaster in Pittsburgh, was a senior at Miami. We had no notes. Just names on a roster. Steve Stone was available to pitch for Miami but didn't.

That day was all a blur to me. Those guys were just names to me. I was awful.

I was much better prepared for my MLB debut. It helped that I was a Pirates fan. I watch Pirates baseball in the summer months. I know the players. But I had to do my homework.

When I entered the broadcast booth at Pittsburgh's PNC Park, I brought along my scorecard from that 1959 game at Wrigley. Costas noted on the air that the scorecard cost 10 cents. He wanted this experience to be fun for me. Before the game, he told me to think of him as my "safety net." I could bring him in at any time and he would make it look like a smooth handoff. I have no doubt he could have done that.

"And hot dogs were 25 cents and they sold four kinds of cigars, from 10 cents to a quarter," I said.

Costas wanted to know if my dad let me smoke one. I was 13 then.

"Nope, not allowed," I said. "He was a high school principal."

In our pregame show, Bob asked how an Indiana boy, with ample reason to cheer for other teams, particularly the Chicago Cubs or White Sox, decided to root for the Pirates.

"Fifty thousand watts of KDKA," I said. "Bob Prince was a colorful announcer…he sold me."

When I called a couple of innings of the exhibition game, I was 40 feet behind home plate and only 20 feet above ground. I was much higher at PNC. I asked some veteran baseball guys if there were any secrets to judging fly balls from my PNC perch. It's one of MLB's highest press boxes.

Most of them said PNC is a difficult place to read the ball off the bat. Their advice was to watch the outfielders' movements.

Costas turned the game over to me in the fourth inning to start my three-inning stint.

"Onto the tightrope I go," I said.

It was a marvelous experience, although I forgot to keep my scorecard current. One of the Cubs smacked a triple and I had mentioned the name of the previous batter getting it. Bob notified me without saying a word, just pointing to his correct scorecard.

I did get to call a home run. Chicago's Miguel Montero, a left-handed catcher, hit one a few rows into the stands in right field. It was an unlikely blast. He was batting .201 after that home run. I think I sold it pretty well. I didn't know off the ball that it was a home run.

My call was: "High and deep. It's gone. And we are tied."

No gimmick. Just a clean, straight call.

At the end of the fifth, I told Costas, off air, "One more inning."

I had been watching the Cubs for a month and had made notes and had done a lot of research and had even called their farm team in Iowa to ask about Kris Bryant and any stories from former Iowa Cubs now with Chicago. I had been prepared. But most of it was spent.

And, though my boys were ahead, I felt it best to have the game back in better hands.

So, after six, Bob took over.

Then, with the Pirates still ahead in the top of the ninth, Costas made good on his commitment to let me shine. He turned over the game to me with three outs to go.

Just my luck, the Pirates immediately found trouble.

But then manager Clint Hurdle brought in closer Mark Melancon. He had 47 saves that season and save No. 27 came in the game I called. He got it done. On a strikeout. The Pirates won 8–4 for their eighth win in their last nine games.

And I was able to say, "Hoist the Jolly Roger…Shoot off the fireworks! Hahr hahr!"

Greg Brown says it "Raise the Jolly Roger." But I'm a hockey guy, and we always say you "hoist" the Stanley Cup.

The Cubs and Pirates played 18 games that season, and the Pirates won four of those games. I am happy to say I called one of those wins.

After the game was finished, I knew I would never call another baseball game. Why would I? This had been the perfect setup. A second game couldn't top this experience.

My other observation is that being a baseball broadcaster must be exhausting. I prepared aggressively. I believed I gathered plenty of information and I used every tidbit and story that I had written on my preparation sheet. I had called three and a half innings of one game. How can these guys keep the information flowing for nine innings and 162 games?

I'm sure other people in my field have given a special gift to a fellow broadcaster. But I cannot imagine anyone gave a fellow broadcaster a gift more precious than the one Costas gave me.

14

CIVIL WAR, 9/11, AND MRS. SUTTER'S POTATO SOUP

Statistics are forgettable, and stories are memorable. That's the way we approach any broadcast at NBC.

It's interesting to note how long a team has gone without a shot or that Pittsburgh's Sidney Crosby has three goals, four assists, and four penalty minutes in the last 37:14 minutes of ice time.

But it's context and personal stories that add even more to a broadcast.

It's difficult to say what traits an aspiring broadcaster will need to be successful, but I can say that curiosity always helps. One of the enjoyable aspects of my job is sitting down with people and hearing about their journey, learning about who helped them, and what they've seen along the way.

A broadcaster's strength is the stories he has collected along the way. I've heard wonderful tales through the years, some happy, some sad, some entertaining, some thought-provoking, but all of them interesting, like the one career minor league defenseman Mike Gaul told me on our way to the 2001 American Hockey League All-Star Game.

Living in Hershey at the time, I had been asked to introduce the All-Stars at the game at Wilkes-Barre/Scranton. I was ride-sharing with Gaul and another player in a station wagon.

Gaul, from Lachine, Quebec, had played for a year at St. Lawrence University before deciding he was better suited to play for the Laval Titan in the Quebec Junior Hockey League. In Laval he played for coach Bob Hartley, who, like Gaul, dreamed of reaching the NHL. They spent two years together, even reaching the Memorial Cup in 1993.

Hartley then set off to coach in the American Hockey League, first in Cornwall, then in Hershey. In the AHL, Hartley learned to live by his wits, trying to confuse other coaches with frequent and prolonged line changes. Referees hated that strategy. It was said that Hartley's games with Cornwall and Hershey would last an extra 10 to 15 minutes.

Meanwhile, Gaul was on his own odyssey. He was with the ECHL Knoxville Cherokees for two seasons, the Timmendorfer Strand in Germany for a year, the Mobile (Alabama) Mysticks for five games, and then three years in Hershey. He played again for Hartley in 1997–98 in Hershey.

By 1998–99, Hartley was coaching with the Colorado Avalanche and Gaul didn't seem to be close to making it.

"I knew the NHL wasn't happening for me," Gaul explained on the ride. "Then, in midseason, my father died. Shortly after I returned from his funeral to the Bears, I got a call from Bob Hartley with our parent team in Colorado. 'We need some help on defense for a game.'"

"What a thrill, after all of those years, I got to be in The Show," he said.

After the game, a 2–1 loss to the San Jose Sharks, Hartley called him into his office.

"I know about your father, Mike," Hartley said to Gaul. "I just thought he should see you play a game in the NHL. I'm sure he liked what he saw tonight."

We can only imagine what Gaul was feeling when Hartley said that.

Gaul played 548 professional games, but he only played two others in the NHL. He played them for the Columbus Blue Jackets the season we traveled together to Wilkes-Barre/Scranton.

But the gift Hartley gave Gaul during the 1998–99 season is one that he will never forget.

Speaking of the Blue Jackets, former NHL coach Ken Hitchcock once gave me the inside story on how the Blue Jackets came to fire off a cannon every time they scored.

When Hitchcock was an assistant with the Philadelphia Flyers, Jack Betson, one of owner Ed Snider's lieutenants, suggested during the All-Star break that Hitchcock should join him on a tour of the Gettysburg battlefield. It's only about 120 miles from Philadelphia.

It became a life-altering visit. Ever the tactician and a proud Canadian, Hitchcock became immersed in U.S. history. On the team bus, he would be seen poring through Civil War magazines. His interest intensified to the point where he would participate in Civil War re-enactments during the off-season.

One fall, I asked him what battles he had relived the previous summer, and he said "Chancellorsville" in such a way that you knew it had not been a joyous experience.

"It may be the last of the series for me," he explained. "The script called for me to die in the first half hour and lie on the battlefield for another three hours. It was cold and rained all day. And you have to lie there until they load you in a cart and haul you off."

But when he didn't stop talking about his re-enactment experiences, you realized that he was far from finished with that phase of his life.

"In the evening they have these large campfires, guys in the grey uniforms are singing 'Dixie' with tears streaming down their cheeks," he said.

Hitchcock always wore the Union blue, something that placed him in a ticklish situation when he went to coach the Dallas Stars. He frequently had some explaining to do about why he didn't dress as a Confederate.

"Texas is in the South," he said in his own defense. "But history shows it was a 'free state.'"

When the coaching carousel took him to Columbus where the team was named the Blue Jackets, his Union ties served him well. Columbus has the "Blue Jackets" nickname because the state of Ohio and Columbus took great pride in sending its husbands and sons to fight for the Union army. Plus, many of the blue jackets worn by union soldiers during the Civil War were manufactured in Columbus.

Hitchcock and another team official took that concept even further when they came up with the idea of shooting a cannon after goals and victories.

The only question was, how would they find a working Civil War cannon?

"We did a search," Hitchcock explained. They discovered there were three actual Civil War cannons still working and for sale. "The prices were too high, so we got in touch with a replica cannon manufacturer in Cincinnati and got one made."

The cannon arrived, and the first order of business along with it—testing out an outdoor cannon inside Nationwide Arena.

"I was in my office one day," he recalled, "and to give you an idea, the charge used on the cannon eventually was a $\frac{1}{16}^{th}$ charge. That day, when they touched it off, they used a ½ charge. Everyone came flying out of their offices not knowing what had happened."

The cannon is now a well-established Blue Jackets tradition, and the blast still startles even if you know it's coming.

Another oddity about the Blue Jackets is that Nationwide Arena is built on the site of the former Ohio State Penitentiary. That means that where Seth Jones, Josh Anderson, and Nick Foligno are sentenced to two minutes in the penalty box for hockey infractions is the same spot where Confederate general John Morgan, gangster "Bugs" Moran, author O. Henry, and members of John Dillinger's gang were incarcerated for their crimes.

I'VE ALWAYS FILED AWAY ODD facts in my memory to use at a later date, such as the story about Chicago Blackhawks goalie Malcolm Subban becoming stuck between floors in an elevator when he was a junior player.

His Belleville Bulls were on a road trip in Sudbury, Ontario, when it happened.

"The elevator said it would hold 10, and there were nine of us," Subban recalled. "We used the phone to alert people. They immediately called the fire department to rescue us."

The length of time it took to rescue them caused some minor panic.

"After about 15 minutes, the oxygen was getting bad and the walls were sweating," Subban said. "We began taking turns ducking to the bottom of the elevator to find oxygen. It took the fire department an hour and a half to get us out of there."

Broadcasters love discovering stories about their sport that aren't well known. It's like winning a church raffle or finding a forgotten $20 bill stuffed in the pocket of a sports coat.

If I asked you to name the only American announcer to broadcast live at the USA–Soviet Union game at the 1980 Olympics in Lake Placid, New York, you would probably say Al Michaels.

But the answer is Sandy Caligiore (pronounced kal-ih-JOHR-ee).

Michaels broadcast live to tape to air later that night on ABC. Caligiore, then 29, was broadcasting live for Saranac Lake's 1,000-watt radio station, WNBZ, 1240 AM. This was the last Olympics for which organizers embraced the tradition of allowing a local station to broadcast live from the events.

If you love hockey and small towns, a visit to Lake Placid should be on your bucket list. It's like visiting Dyersville, Iowa, and seeing the Field of Dreams.

I didn't work at those 1980 Olympics, but thanks to listening to Caligiore's story I have a sense of what the scene was like. The population of Lake Placid was 2,500 when it hosted the Olympics in 1932 and it was the same when the city was host in 1980. When you go to Lake Placid, what you get is a picturesque-beyond-description blend of mountains, winding brooks, ski jumps, and courteous people interwoven into the fabric of hockey.

"Directly above the rink and the speed skating oval is Lake Placid High School," Caligiore told me. "They gave the kids five weeks off and the high school became the press center. Our station was given a studio on the third floor."

What I've been told is that ABC wanted to move the game from its scheduled 5:00 PM starting time to 8:00 PM because then it could be broadcast live in prime time. But the Soviet delegation balked because then it would have been on at 4:00 AM in Russia.

The game stayed at 5:00 and most Americans didn't see it until prime time on tape. As a result, plenty knew the score before Michaels uttered his famous line: "Do you believe in miracles?"

Some people in upper New York were able to see the game broadcast live by Canada's CBC. But some of them, maybe several hundred, received the news of Mike Eruzione scoring the winning goal delivered to them by Caligiore on WNBZ. He is now the answer to a trivia question that will stump the most knowledgeable of sports fans. His color analyst was Tom Fisch, a local schoolteacher.

Caligiore told me he didn't start thinking the Americans could win until the final minutes of the game.

"There was so much time remaining after the Eruzione goal," Caligiore said. "But in the final minutes, the Soviets weren't getting much zone time, and they never pulled [goalie Vladimir] Myshkin. This told us they were completely unprepared for a close game and had no idea how to react. At that point, I knew a miracle was possible."

He said to this day he doesn't understand why the Soviets pulled famed goaltender Vladislav Tretiak in favor of Myshkin.

One irony of Caligiore's status as the lone "live" American broadcaster was that his station was obligated to reduce power to 250 watts at sunset, per FCC policy. Thus, Caligiore likely had fewer listeners when Eruzione scored than he did when the game started.

Not that Caligiore had any time to ponder that. "There was work to do when the game ended, as we were covering other competitions as well," he recalled.

When people were leaving Lake Placid the day after the Olympics ended, Caligiore finally had time to reflect.

"I got up, had breakfast, and went into our bathroom to shave," he recalled. "I looked in the mirror and just began crying. It had all finally hit me...no matter what I did the rest of my career, no matter where I ended up, in or out of hockey, nothing would ever come close to the magnitude of that event."

Caligiore worked for the U.S. ski team and then the luge team and attended multiple Olympics. But none compared to the Lake Placid Games, when his broadcast was the only live American broadcast of the greatest sports triumph the sports world has ever seen.

As Paul Harvey used to say, now you know the rest of the story.

I'VE BEEN AROUND LONG ENOUGH that I have a story about Mickey Mouse, and I'm not talking about the day Disney agreed to own the Mighty Ducks NHL expansion team.

I'm talking about November 19, 1983, when I called the Edmonton Oilers' 13–4 shellacking of the Devils in Edmonton.

Wayne Gretzky had eight points in that game. He should have celebrated one of the top offensive performances in NHL history. Instead, Gretzky, out of character, attacked the Devils organization.

"It got to the point where it wasn't even funny," Gretzky said. "How long has it been for them? Three years? Five? Seven? Probably closer to nine. Well, it's about time they got their act together. They're ruining the whole league. They better stop running a Mickey Mouse organization and put somebody on the ice. I feel damn sorry for [Devils goalies] Ron Low and Chico Resch."

Low had played with the Oilers before coming to the Devils, and he was one of Gretzky's friends. That may explain Gretzky's rant.

The phrase "Mickey Mouse organization" flew around the hockey world at warp speed. Gretzky apologized but couldn't un-ring the bell.

This was a disaster that everyone saw coming. The Edmonton Oilers were a powerhouse, loaded with young, talented future Hall of Famers—Paul Coffey (22), Glenn Anderson (22), Grant Fuhr (21), Jari Kurri (23), Mark Messier (23), and Wayne Gretzky (23).

The Devils were 2–17 going into that game. They posted one win in October (against the Detroit Red Wings) and one in November (against the Blackhawks).

Low sat across from me at breakfast that morning and said, "I just hope we don't get embarrassed tonight."

It was such an odd night. Devils GM and coach Billy MacMillan decided he would watch the game from the press box, hoping he would see something from above that would help him fix the team.

My broadcast partner Mike Eruzione was also not at his usual station. His role with ABC-TV at the upcoming Sarajevo Olympics required him to be away for the weekend. MSG had airlifted in Rangers analyst John Davidson, another MSG employee, to work with me. It was the first of many outings together.

It was a game to forget. Although the Devils scored twice in the first 3:07 to take a 2–0 lead, the Oilers got rolling with four of their own in the first and four more in the second.

Glenn "Chico" Resch replaced Low. He remembered skating over to the bench with the score 12–4 and the Devils on the power play with three minutes left in the game, and saying: "Boys, let's just not get scored on."

But Edmonton sent out Gretzky and Anderson to kill the penalty and they generated a goal on a 2-on-0 breakaway. Gretzky finished the night with three goals and five assists.

MacMillan was fired after that loss. Max McNab became general manager and Tom McVie was picked to be the coach.

As fate would have, the Oilers came to New Jersey two months later. The barn was packed with people, many carrying signs and Mickey Mouse balloons.

The Oilers won 5–4, but it was a much better game. The two teams also tied 3–3 later in the season.

THROUGH THE YEARS, I'VE HEARD many stories of perseverance, but none better than the one of NHLer Pat Verbeek developing into a 40-goal scorer after his thumb was cut off in a farming accident.

It happened after Verbeek's third season with the Devils, on May 15, 1985, while Pat was working on the family farm in Petrolia, Ontario, not far across the Blue Water Bridge from Port Huron.

While loading a corn planting machine, Pat reached to grab a piece of paper to prevent it from clogging up the gears. But he reached too far, and his left hand became caught in the auger. It cut off his thumb and cut other fingers as well.

Out of immediate shock, Pat's brother, Brian, got on the walkie-talkie and told their parents, Gerard and Joanne, what had happened. Then the brothers jumped into a nearby truck and gunned it for the hospital in Sarnia. Pat bled into a Kleenex box on the way there.

No cell phones in those days. But the parents quickly drove out to the corn planter and searched the bins feverishly for the severed thumb until it was located.

"Don't sew him up," they said on a phone call to the hospital. "We're coming in with the thumb."

Pat recalls he was wobbly when he arrived at the hospital. Too much blood had been lost. He was probably in shock as he walked down the hallway in the emergency room.

His parents walked in carrying the thumb a few minutes later.

After the thumb was reattached by surgery, there was no blood flow to it. Out of frustration, the doctor took a ballpoint pen out of his pocket and flipped the thumb with it.

As if the pen had been a magic wand, the blood began to flow. The thumb's pinkish color returned. After two weeks in a hospital room, set at 95 degrees to keep the blood thin, Pat was released. It was June then. He went to Devils training camp in September, and boy did he have a story to tell.

He scored 25 goals that next season and went on to score 40 or more four times. His career spanned two decades. He won a Stanley Cup with Dallas in 1999 and finished with 522 career goals.

For perspective, know that in the NHL's 102 years, 7,190 players have appeared in at least one game. Only 36 have more goals than Pat Verbeek. Thirty of those players are in the Hall of Fame.

Now that's perseverance.

I'VE MET MANY INTERESTING PEOPLE during my career, none more colorful than Paul Stewart, the former World Hockey Association (WHA) and NHL tough guy and NHL referee.

During the 1978–79 season, I was sitting in my Maine Mariners office after our morning skate in preparation for a night game against the visiting Philadelphia Firebirds. After the Firebirds finished their skate, they walked up a ramp, past our offices, and out the double doors for a short walk to the Holiday Inn. That's where nearly every visiting team stayed.

On this day, one Firebird paused on the ramp and began talking to me. I recognized it was Boston-born Stewart.

A year earlier, the WHA's Quebec Nordiques had sent Stewart to the Binghamton (New York) Broome Dusters, when it was their minor league affiliate.

The "return of Stewie" to the AHL was heralded in the newspaper like he was Douglas MacArthur returning to the Philippines. Many fans remembered Stewart's past fighting glory for the Dusters (1975–77) when they were in the North American Hockey League.

John Paddock, a future NHL coach, was a 30-goal scorer with 275 penalty minutes that season. I recall Paddock reading a Charlie Jaworski article about Stewart in the Binghamton newspaper, casually folding up the newspaper and proclaiming: "Looks like this is going to be a nut show tonight."

As it turned out, it wasn't. Waiting for Stewart to stir up trouble, I was prepared for almost anything, but not for what he did first.

One of Maine's defensemen was holding the puck behind the net when Stewart came down the ice on a forecheck. Instead of chasing him behind the net, Stewart jumped Superman-style, stomach-first, onto the net.

The Mariners goalie had sidestepped the airborne Stewart, leaving him hanging over the net, theatrically and uselessly sweeping his stick one-handedly toward the defenseman. There was no way from that distance he could reach the puck. It was a funny maneuver and fans applauded Stewie's effort.

When I had talked to Stewart, he didn't seem like an out-of-control fighter. We had a sane conversation about growing up around Boston, his time at the University of Pennsylvania, and what he was doing with the Firebirds. He is very likeable.

His main objective that night was to do something the Philadelphia Flyers would notice. He was hoping Flyers GM Keith Allen would want his fighting skills for the Broad Street Bullies. Stewart wanted to be in the NHL. As fate would have it, Allen and Flyers owner Ed Snider were both scheduled to attend the Mariners game that night.

I pieced together the rest of the story from conversations with Firebirds players. Before the game, Stewart made it clear that he planned to challenge the Mariners and his new teammates didn't like that plan. Fighting the Maine Mariners—the AHL's most penalized team—was not what other Phantoms wanted to do.

The word spread that "if Stewie wants to start something, he's on his own."

When the Mariners took a decisive lead, Stewart immediately challenged Maine tough guy Glen Cochrane. It didn't go well for Stewart. Meanwhile, Stewart's new teammates sat back and did nothing. Then Stewart went after Maine's other top heavyweight, southpaw Jim Cunningham. Stewart lost that one too. In that bout he was bloodied to the point of needing repairs. He went into the dressing room to get them because there was not enough time remaining in the third period to serve his penalties.

After the game, Allen, Snider, and some of us staff members were invited for a postgame dinner at the very popular DiMillo's restaurant in Portland. Mariners coach Pat Quinn was there as well. Everyone was talking about Stewart.

"I felt sorry for that one kid," Snider said. "And no one helped him out."

That was a no-no in the Philadelphia Flyers organization.

The following season, Quebec was no longer a WHA franchise. They were in the NHL and Stewart was an NHL player.

When Stewart traveled with the Nordiques for the first time to the Boston Garden, the place where Stewart played and watched games as a kid, he wanted to make a splash.

"Stewart comes up to Wayne Cashman and asks, 'Who are the three toughest guys on your team?'" former Bruins player Peter McNab told me. "So 'Cash' tells him—John Wensink, Terry O'Reilly, and Stan Jonathan. The guy says 'Thanks' and skates away. And those were the three guys he fought that night."

At the time, I was still with the Mariners. But it was Thanksgiving and we were off that night. I watched the Bruins-Nordiques on Channel 38 as the game unfolded. And, systematically, Stewart fought all three Bruins. After each of the first two fights, he went directly to the penalty box. You could tell he knew to watch for the television camera red lights to go on because he had seen enough Bruins games on television. Stewart knew the network always showed one combatant and then the other in the penalty boxes. When the light went on and the camera was on him, Stewart waved.

The third fight with Jonathan was different. Jonathan was tossed for having a cast or metal guard on his wrist and fighting with it. Stewart was cut. Both were out—Stewart for his third fighting major. He exited past the Bruins' bench and then down a small flight of stairs to the Nordiques dressing room.

The camera followed him as he disappeared. And then, as if he had forgotten something, he reappeared and gave one last smile and wave.

Reportedly, the next day he went down and threw his skates in Boston's Charles River.

"I've done it all," he supposedly said.

After 12 years as a player, including 21 games in the NHL, he retired and eventually became an NHL referee. He had a long and colorful officiating career, and one of the highlights was the final game in old Boston Garden. It was a preseason game between the Bruins and Montreal Canadiens. Paul Stewart asked for, and received permission, to be the referee.

At that point, Stewart truly had done it all. In 2018, he was inducted into the U.S. Hockey Hall of Fame.

I HAVE FOUND HISTORICAL NOTES can also be a broadcaster's good friend, like the fact that as late as the 1950s the NHL only had three referees because it only had six teams. Every referee worked on Saturday nights when every team played.

No supervisor. Little security.

"We would have to fight our way out of places like Chicago Stadium with only one cop to keep order," said Bill Chadwick, who was one of three referees in the 1950s.

Officials had no identity until 1951, when they were given striped shirts and numbers. Referees had the orange armband.

In 1977, the NHL put officials' names on their backs, but they went back to numbers only in 1993 when everyone agreed that anonymity was more beneficial for officials.

Rather than letting the numbers signify seniority, NHL officials agreed to let officials pick their numbers. Officials are forbidden to wear No. 1.

Kerry Fraser picked No. 2, saying in his house his wife was No. 1 and he was No. 2. Terry Gregson chose No. 4; his favorite player growing up was Red Kelly, who wore that number. Rob Shick picked No. 16 because that was the number he wore on a championship baseball team. Dan O'Halloran chose No. 13 because he felt he had been lucky. As a young man, on a visit to Detroit, he was the victim of a random drive-by shooting. He was unaware he had been hit until he spied the bullet on the floor of his buddy's car. Fortunately, the bullet entered his back without hitting any vital organs. Several Olympics and Stanley Cup Finals later, he announced the 2019–20 season would be his last.

Another favorite historical note is that while Jacques Plante made the goalie mask legitimate in the NHL by wearing one in 1959, the first goalie to wear one on a regular basis was Elizabeth Graham (Queen's University Golden Gaels, Kingston, Ontario). She was urged by her father to wear a fencing mask to protect her face.

I've also always enjoyed the notes I gather to speak to the small-town roots of hockey. For example, I remember former NHL player Brooks Laich (Wawota, Saskatchewan, population 591) telling me that he played outdoor hockey when the temperature was 40 below zero. Wawota had multiple churches, a general store, and one bar. Laich said the Dakota native Canadian tribe named the city many years earlier; it means "lots of snow."

Laich is not from the smallest Canadian town. Far from it. Travis Moen (Stewart Valley, Saskatchewan, population 100) and Brad Richards (Murray Harbour, Nova Scotia, population 300) are both Stanley Cup winners.

Another favorite story in my collection involves legendary minor league tough guys Archie Henderson and Gary Rissling. They couldn't have been more different in terms of physical presence. Archie was 6-foot-6 and Rissling was 5-foot-9, but you wouldn't want to tangle with either man.

They became teammates in 1977–78, playing for my old boss Morris Snider in Port Huron. This was after I had moved on to Portland in the AHL.

Henderson and Rissling were teammates the following season with the Hershey Bears, and both passed Nelson Burton's Hershey Bears record of 323 penalty minutes in a season. Rissling had 333, Henderson 325.

Both wanted the record by himself. It would come down to the final game of the regular season against New Haven. Whoever had the most penalty minutes would have the record.

"There was a little bit of tension on the bus," Henderson told me later about the day.

The official scoresheet from the game shows that Rissling had two for roughing in the first period and a delay of game call in the second. Henderson had nothing through 40 minutes.

Henderson picked up the story from there.

"In the last minute of the game, one of our defensemen played the puck up the boards right in front of our bench," Henderson said. "I grabbed him, dragged him over the boards, and took his place. As luck would have it, Frank Beaton was on the ice for New Haven, so I went after him. By dropping my gloves, I knew I had five. But I needed more."

Henderson knew if he kept fighting after they were separated, he would pile up the penalty minutes.

"I just kept throwing 'em," Henderson said. "The ref warned me, but I kept it up."

Henderson's penalty-minute assessment in the final minute was 15. More importantly, Rissling didn't have time to get another shift in.

"Gary and I almost got into a fight on the way to the dressing room," Henderson said.

The weird aspect of the story is that the official records ended up showing both Rissling and Henderson with 337 minutes. Odder still, the official statistics, calculated by hand in those days, showed both men had the same number of minutes, majors, minors, misconducts, etc.

That seemed to be an unlikely coincidence. When Henderson first told me the story 20 years ago, I contacted legendary Hershey Bears coach and general manager Frank Mathers. He kept newspaper articles in a large scrapbook in that era.

He read me the account that had been reported in the newspaper. It verified Henderson's memory of what happened.

Since those numbers were recorded by hand, it's obvious that there was a duplication error.

The Hershey reporter Steve Summers covered all of them, and his account had Henderson with more minutes.

"Which would you believe?" Mathers asked me.

I told him I believed Henderson and Summers. I still do today.

NOT EVERY STORY AND MEMORY can be as entertaining or as fun as the Stewart tale or the Henderson-Rissling rivalry.

But some stories are too important to forget or not to retell.

On September 11, 2001, I was sitting in St. Clair, Michigan, listening to the ABC radio news when Doug Limerick reported that "a plane has crashed into the World Trade Center."

I immediately thought it must have been accidental, probably a takeoff gone wrong. Shortly after Limerick's newscast ended, he was quickly back on again.

It was no accident.

Because I'm an older American, I now have a second date that I won't ever forget.

September 11, 2001, was added to November 22, 1963, as dates that are indelible in my memory. On both days, there was an attack, an American tragedy, and another faction that took maddening pleasure with the result.

I was in high school, sitting in Bob Dawes' psychology class, when it was announced that President John F. Kennedy had been assassinated. Because our school had no television, our principal, Dr. Sherman Waggoner, explained the details of Kennedy's death. Minutes later, school was dismissed.

I still struggle watching replays of the scene in Dallas, of Jack Ruby's killing of Lee Harvey Oswald, and of almost any video from September 11. There is a revulsion and an urge to look away.

We have been conditioned to happy endings and believing the holiday lyric that states, "The wrong shall fail, the right prevail, and peace on earth, good will to men."

But we know it doesn't work that way. I like to collect stories and bring them out at a future date. But you don't easily find a way to tell what happened in the NHL on September 11. We lost two Los Angeles Kings scouts, Mark Bavis and Garnet "Ace" Bailey, who were on one of the planes that slammed into one of the Twin Towers.

Another story I remember from that day was one about a gallant firefighter. Firefighting must have been in the family DNA. He had three sons who were firefighters. He lost one that day. But he said his faith was strengthened.

"We call fire 'the devil,'" he said. "We fought the devil that day and we saved a lot of people."

He added that he felt God was all around and that God was there, fighting the devil with him and his teammates.

Retired ex-Islander Jean Potvin was across the street in his office and had clear sight of the attack.

And there was a guy I've known for nearly 40 years. A bearded hockey fan named "Fuzzy." Took years for me to learn his last name, Cohen. I first met him in New Haven. He would take bus trips to hockey games. He went to games in almost every league, and anywhere a Greyhound could take him.

A passionate hockey fan, his day job was that of a courier. On that morning, the sky was blue, and the world seemed right. Fuzzy Cohen arrived early to make his delivery at the Twin Towers. Since he was early, he took a seat on one of the benches outside to read the sports page of the *New York Post*.

He saw it all happen.

New Jersey Devils forward Randy McKay didn't see anything, but he will always remember where he was on September 11, 2001. He was one of my favorite Devils. When New Jersey was winning its first Stanley Cup in 1995, he led the Stanley Cup playoffs in scoring for a while. He was a throwback player. Ginseng in coffee, a raspy voice, a presence, with a hammering scoring punch on the famed "Crash Line" with Bobby Holik and Mike Peluso.

By September 11, 2001, he had two Stanley Cup titles. But that wasn't important as he boarded a plane at Newark Airport to attend a funeral for a family member.

Shortly after 9:00 AM, he was asked to disembark. Four planes took off from the East Coast that morning and terrorists forced them to crash. Many passengers were killed. McKay isn't going to forget where he was that morning.

Initially, stocks spiked down, church and campus chapel attendance spiked up. Wall Street, located a couple of blocks away from the Twin Towers, recovered. A memorial was created. Bin Laden was killed. And any American over 20 likely received a revision on what mattered.

SOME STORIES I COLLECT I don't use as often during my broadcasts, even though they are often more important than many I do use.

One quote we see often is "Adversity doesn't build character. It reveals it."

Some view it as a cliché. But clichés are clichés because they are truths that continue to repeat themselves. Many clichés, like the one on adversity, can speak truth at the lowest times in a person's life.

In the spring of 2014, the New York Rangers finished second in the Metropolitan Division, 13 points behind the Pittsburgh Penguins.

The Penguins and Rangers finished the month of April by disposing of stubborn geographic rivals in the first round of the NHL playoffs. It took the powerful Penguins six games to dispose of Columbus. Two days later, the Rangers outdueled the Flyers at Madison Square Garden, 2–1, in Game 7.

And when they faced one another in the second round, it looked as if the regular season dominance was going to continue for the firm of Crosby, Fleury, and Malkin. They excelled through the first four games of the series, winning three of them while allowing only five goals.

But, as we all gathered in Pittsburgh, preparing for Game 5, wondering if we were headed for the traditional post-playoff handshake line, tragedy struck.

France St. Louis, mother of Rangers winger Martin St. Louis, died in Laval, Quebec, of a heart attack. She was only 63. Immediately, St. Louis left the team to join his father, sister, and grieving family members. But on the afternoon of Game 5 in Pittsburgh, less than 24 hours after he left the team, St. Louis was back to play.

"The family said this is what she would have wanted," coach Alain Vigneault told us at a pregame press conference.

St. Louis also asked for privacy about this matter. What he didn't need at the time was nearly 100 members of the media listening to what would have been a difficult press conference. We all understood. He would suit up and play and we would let him say what he wanted to say when he wanted to say it.

There was something deeply buried in my mind about these awful circumstances.

As a Pittsburgh Pirates fans since 1959, I recalled something about the last of the Pirates' World Series teams. I called Kent Tekulve, the closer on the 1979 team.

"We were trailing Baltimore in the World Series, three games to one," he said. "I was driving to Three Rivers Stadium on the day of Game 5 when I heard on the radio that the mother of our manager, Chuck Tanner, had died.

"Many things are going through your mind as you hear that on the way to the ballpark, including, 'I wonder if he will come in today,' and 'If he does, what do we say to him?'

"As a team, we were suited up in the clubhouse, sort of standing on one leg and then the other, trying to think of something to say, when the door to his office opened and he came out."

On the verge of elimination, Tanner was both emotional and determined.

"My mom *is* a Pirates fan," he began. "She knows we're in trouble, and she's gone ahead to get us some help."

Tanner walked back into his office and prepared for that day's game.

What effect did that have?

"If it would have been 'Let's win this one for Chuck's mom,' we would have won Game 5, gone on to Baltimore and lost Game 6, and come home," Tekulve said. "But the thought now was, 'If he's able to come here to work with this kind of load, how can we do any less?'"

The baseball team's identity song was Sister Sledge's "We Are Family." And they won the next three. Tekulve was on the mound when the celebration began in Baltimore following the 27th out of Game 7.

Still a Pittsburgh resident and a Penguins fan (closers and goalies, he says, are a lot alike), Tekulve asked me if St. Louis said anything to the team as Tanner did before Game 5.

"Don't know, but let me ask," I said.

"I'd appreciate knowing," Tekulve said. "I know how we didn't know what to say and Chuck helped us by speaking first."

In April 2015, nearly a year after the death of his mom, I sat next to St. Louis in the Rangers locker room and asked the question.

"All I said was, 'Guys, she's going to get us some bounces,'" St. Louis said. "'Just watch. She's going to get some for us.'"

Short speech. Just like Tanner's.

"And then we won in Pittsburgh 5–1," St. Louis said. "Big decisive win for our team. And Game 6 was on Mother's Day in New York. On the first goal, Fleury blocked a shot, I was near the net, and it bounced off me into the net. I didn't touch it. It touched me. I wanted the puck because it meant so much, and after it went in it bounced right back to me, so I picked it up."

230

The Rangers of 2014 never trailed Pittsburgh after that. They won the Mother's Day game 3–1 (St. Louis was the first star), went back to Pittsburgh and won Game 7 on a 2–1 decision.

The conference final series opened in Montreal with an imposing Rangers win over the host Canadiens, 7–2. St. Louis had the first of the seven goals and an assist. The following day, the entire team gathered to attend France St. Louis' funeral at Sainte-Dorothee Catholic Church in nearby Laval.

Teammate Brad Richards said before the funeral, "Marty's done an unbelievable job keeping everything together and helping his sister and his dad get through this. You wouldn't expect anything else."

Teammate Ryan McDonough summarized St. Louis' eulogy of his mother: "He shared a couple of the good memories with us. You could just tell she was a great lady and influenced him a lot."

Then, sparked by an overtime winner from St. Louis in Game 4 of the conference final, his third goal of the series, the Rangers reached the Stanley Cup Final for the first time in 20 years.

Though they lost that series to the Los Angeles Kings in five games—the equivalent of six with 69 minutes of overtime—there had been something inspirational about watching a team facing elimination win eight more games before the summer.

It is amateur theology on my part. Hockey players don't talk about faith much. It's not that they don't have it, it's just that they recognize it's personal, and theirs is a culture where there are plenty of people who point a finger at hypocrisy. Even the most devout person makes mistakes. But it's adversity that reveals much. It did with the Pirates in 1979, and the Rangers of 2014.

"My mom was a person of great faith," St. Louis said.

Importance of family is a theme in the NHL. Bobby, Dennis, and Bobby's son, Brett. Gordie Howe and his sons, Mark and Marty. Tony and Phil Esposito. Pete and Frank Mahovlich. Maurice and Henri Richard. Keith Tkachuk and his sons, Matthew and Brady. The Bentley brothers. The Staals. I could go on a long time.

But the symbol of the NHL's family values is the Sutter family of Viking, Alberta (population, 1,041). The six Sutter brothers (Brian, Darryl, Brent, Duane, and twins Rich and Ron) won eight Stanley Cups between them. The other non-NHL son, Gary, won the Alberta Lottery.

In 2007, the Devils played December 21 in Edmonton and had another game scheduled for December 23 in Calgary. My analyst Glenn "Chico" Resch proposed we travel to Calgary by car and make a side trip to Viking to see the Sutters' 300-acre spread. Having phoned ahead, Resch said he and I, plus MSG-TV host Steve Cangialosi, were going to be Grace Sutter's guests for lunch. She was 71 at the time.

When we showed up, a huge pot of potato soup was bubbling up on the same stove on which she used to cook three meals a day for her boys.

While the soup was cooking, a neighbor gave us a tour of the Sutter homestead, where calves were still being raised. The frozen ground told us that planting season was still more than four months away.

In the barn's hayloft, hockey nets were set up at both ends. Sticks and pucks had been left right where they were dropped when it was time for chores or supper. The Sutter boys told us later that they played "barn hockey," which was like street hockey only played on the second floor.

Lunch was uneventful, just cheerful conversation with a loving woman who didn't mind retelling stories about her boys that she had told 1,000 times before.

"Richard and Ronald used to switch desks just to fool the teachers," she said.

Photos. Memorabilia. Sticks. Trophies. Her home was a museum to a storied hockey family.

I felt such a peace and serenity visiting the Sutter home. I've told people many times that the brief visit in Viking was one of the favorite days of my career. Like the character Terence Mann (played by James Earl Jones) said in the movie *Field of Dreams*, I felt like I had been "dipped in magic waters."

15

CAN YOU BEAM ME TO ANAHEIM?

A few years ago, coach Joel Quenneville sat in his office at the United Center following the Chicago Blackhawks' morning skate. Laptop on the desk in front of him. Cigar humidor in front of the computer.

He was a relaxed coach, the kind of relaxed that comes from winning three Stanley Cups with the same team.

As a broadcaster you always like to talk to a coach on the day of a game because you want, and need, an understanding of what has been happening with his team. How are the power play and penalty kill performing? Are they scoring enough? Are there any players who are playing a more prominent role? How are the line combinations working?

But you also want to talk to him because you hope to find a story or two that your viewers haven't heard about the team or the coach. Everything that comes out of your mouth can't be about the Xs and Os or your broadcast will be uninspiring.

On this day, I asked how important morning skates are to a player and a coach. Then, I asked him to talk about the worst travel experience he ever had in the NHL.

Bingo.

When you are an interviewer, you never know what question will elicit the best information. In this case, it was definitely the question about travel that caused Quenneville to perk up.

"Oh, the Hartford flight to Montreal," Quenneville said. "Not even close. The absolute worst and the scariest."

It was February in 1984, and Quenneville was a Hartford Whalers defenseman. The Whalers had chartered a Convair 580 for a flight to Montreal to play the Canadiens the next night.

Because the Convair holds 32 to 50 passengers, the Whalers invited some office staff and sponsors to fly with the players and coaches.

Everyone looks forward to visiting Montreal because it is such a cosmopolitan city, with exquisite restaurants and plentiful shopping. The Montreal Forum was still the Canadiens' home and a trip to that venue was one of the wonders of the world for a hockey fan.

According to Quenneville, the Convair 580 flew best at 13,000 feet and unfortunately that was also the exact location of the center of a blizzard that was controlling the skies that night.

The plane bounced and pitched through the turbulence. The pilot had no alternative except to ride out the storm. The rough air took its toll on the passengers. Everyone was nauseous, and some were vomiting. The situation went from dicey to critical. When the Convair 580 was 100 miles south of Montreal, the Dorval Airport control tower informed the pilot he could not land there. The runway had just been closed because it was covered by 18 inches of snow.

Fear was evident in the cabin. Where could they land?

"They told us Ottawa to the west was still open," Whalers broadcaster Chuck Kaiton told me. "But as we headed there, they let us know Ottawa was now closed. And, worse, we only had two hours of fuel left."

The pilot only had one alternative. He headed home. The plane pitched and rattled all the way to Bradley Airport outside Hartford with only 30 minutes of fuel to spare.

General manager Emile Francis immediately walked to the pay telephone (no cell phones back then) to call the Canadiens to let them know there would be no opponent.

"Emile gets Serge Savard on the phone," Kaiton said. "And Serge says, 'We're in luck. They just re-opened Dorval. Give it another try.'"

Chuck didn't hear what Francis said in response, but he can guess what was said. Everyone on the plane was shaken.

"There would not be another try that day," Kaiton said.

Added Kaiton: "It was the worst. We were all glad to get off and most everyone was sick."

The last word was Quenneville's: "All the barf bags were full."

Don't mind saying that I say a quick prayer for the crew flying the aircraft before takeoff and landing on every flight I take.

With the many years I've been flying for my job, I never had an experience that came close to being that terrifying. The worst that happened to me was that I was inconvenienced.

The most challenging delay I ever had came when I was the Devils broadcaster. We had a blizzard in Ottawa after a game and a day off before our next game in Pittsburgh. We didn't travel with the team; the Devils had already left. Our original flight plan called for us to fly from Ottawa to Toronto to Pittsburgh. But flight after flight to Toronto was canceled the next day. Some of our crew rented a van and started driving to Pittsburgh. They crossed into the United States in Buffalo and arrived in Pittsburgh sometime after midnight following a harrowing 12-hour drive.

For those of us who stayed patient, a flight was allowed to leave in the late afternoon. We stayed at a Toronto airport hotel and caught a flight to Pittsburgh on game day.

The only time I had any measure of fear while traveling occurred when I was traveling by bus with the Port Huron Flags. After driving from Muskegon, Michigan, to Port Huron, a trip of only 219 miles, we hit a slick patch of ice just before we pulled into Port Huron. The bus went into a three-direction skid. We were humming along at a normal speed, and suddenly the back end started sliding in a different direction.

The driver corrected and suddenly the spin was going the opposite direction. Coach Bob McCammon always sat up front, and within seconds he was passing me and headed toward the back of the bus. I immediately wondered whether I should be doing the same. But the driver gained control after the third spin and got us back on track. It was only fearful for several seconds.

The only other bus issue I ever had was a breakdown on the way from Port Huron to Flint. It was the Flags' shortest trip, just over an hour. There was no concern because we had time to call for another bus if necessary.

But it didn't come to that because one of our players, Danny Newman, was a trained diesel mechanic. This was the same Newman who signed a contract with the bus running on opening day. This was an era when players had off-season jobs and he knew about engines.

I remember him jumping off the bus, lifting up the cover on the side, and his upper torso disappearing into the engine.

He climbed back aboard, the bus turned over nicely. "You got to grease these things," he said before retaking his seat.

I've had some fun travel experiences, like the time in 2008 when Sam Flood chartered a bus for a short trip we had from Detroit to Pittsburgh after a matinee game in Detroit during the Stanley Cup Final.

Drawing on our *Slap Shot* memories, someone said "we should get a sledgehammer and make the bus mean."

Our bus driver didn't entirely understand the reference, but it was fun nonetheless. We stopped at the last rest area on the Ohio Turnpike and dined on McDonald's hamburgers and fries. It felt like a school field trip, with a good time had by all. We only went by bus for one game. It is a pleasant memory.

In 2007, Sam chartered a plane for us during the Ottawa-Pittsburgh series. My memory of that is our small jet landing in a tiny terminal in Pittsburgh and Eddie Olczyk rushing out to crouch in front of a television to watch the Kentucky Derby.

Eddie likes to urge on the horses he bets on.

As I recall, Eddie did well. But what I really remember is Eddie telling me he had come exceptionally close to hitting on a trifecta. Eddie knows his horses.

"If that would have come in, I could have paid for the charter back to Ottawa," he said.

The truth is that I don't enjoy the travel associated with my job. After seven years of riding buses in the minor leagues, I had enough. The 14-hour trips from Port Huron to Des Moines and Portland to Halifax had made me look forward to reaching the NHL, where planes are the preferred mode of transportation. But after 40 years of air travel, with the last 18 done under very necessary post 9/11 security conditions, I now say that travel is the only difficult aspect of my job.

As much as I enjoyed broadcasting USA star T.J. Oshie's shootout heroics against Russia at the 2014 Olympics in Sochi, Russia, the memory of that experience is diminished by the difficulty I had with sleep deprivation. I had sleeping issues when I arrived there and when I returned home. Even at the 1998 Olympics in Nagano, I had trouble. It took me a week to adjust when I arrived in Japan and 10 days to return to normal when I was back home.

The Olympics I enjoyed the most were the 2010 Games, because travel was easy. The time difference was only three hours, Joyce came with me, and the competition was incredible. The Canada-U.S. gold medal games in both men's and women's hockey will remain with me forever. Calling Sidney Crosby's goal that won the gold medal was one of my career highlights.

Not only was there no jet lag at the Vancouver Olympics, but I slept fine. Even broadcasting many, many games, I felt energized. Having Joyce there certainly helped.

She attended one of the U.S. women's hockey games and also had a day of figure skating at the old Pacific Coliseum.

After Canada's gold medal men's hockey victory, I had free time. Joyce and I attended the closing ceremony together. It was a lifetime memory for both of us to be a part of such pageantry.

I have been told that sleep is harder to come by as you grow older, and I have found that to be true. After the Sochi Games, I whispered to myself, "This is it. There won't be another one of these for me."

The next Games were the 2018 Games in Korea and I knew that would be a nightmare for me when it came to sleep. NBC was gracious enough to let me skip those games. Between my agent, Lou Oppenheim, and Sam Flood, they have succeeded in extending my career by easing my travel concerns.

If I could beam up from Montreal to Anaheim like the *Star Trek* characters do, I could broadcast indefinitely. But unfortunately, that only happens on TV and in the movies.

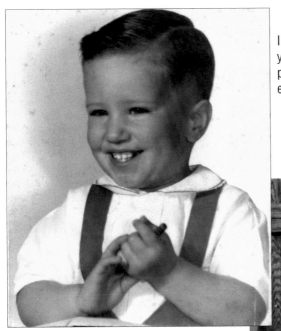

I was around three years old in this picture. Ice cream just entered the room.

My brother, Dan (left), around age eight. I was about five. As usual, a dog is nearby.

Our gang in recess football, with the ill-fated LaFontaine school in the background.

My parents, Charles and Florence, on their wedding day, May 10, 1941, 18½ years before their (and my) first live hockey game.

The House (after we moved from LaFontaine). Just out of view on the right is the left-field fence, 157 feet from home plate.

Uh, *The Wonder Years*? Eighth grade.

Getting the "first degree" (a bachelor's degree at Manchester) with President A. Blair Helman.

Spinning the dials at WBAT in Marion, Indiana. A steady dose of Tony Bennett, Mantovani, and Bert Kaempfert.

My first team, the 1973–74 Port Huron Wings of the IHL, where I'm sporting a clip-on bow tie. Only one team missed the playoffs in a nine-team league: us!

Family at Christmas: Dan, Dad, Mom, and me. Present but not pictured: numerous dogs, cats, goats, and sheep.

Bill Clement reads letters from fans during a Flyers broadcast in 1990.

Eddie Olczyk and I laughing again—a lot of that in 14 years, and one winning 50/50 raffle ticket.

Surrounded by legends: Nos. 87, 66, 4, myself, 99, and 19 at All-Star Weekend in Los Angeles, 2017.

(Above) Living a dream: a Bucs baseball broadcast from PNC with Bob Costas. And we won! (Left) Living a dream II: Pirates Fantasy Camp in 2012. Just like my hero, Bill Mazeroski (but no cigar and no hands).

(Top) Our beloved Katie. (Above left) Liberty Anne I (left) and Poochie Dan (neither bothered the hydrant). (Above right) Liberty Anne II (left) and Joy Bells.

The Hoosier Nerd outkicked his coverage with Joyce Anne. (Top left) Day 1. (Top right) With Joyce's best ever equine friend, Proclaim My Fame, award-winning cutting horse and a real gentle giant. (Above) Year 40.

16

LIFE WITH THE PEACOCK

One major benefit of the family's move from Wabash, Indiana, countryside in 1957, was that the NBC affiliate in Fort Wayne, Channel 33, arrived much clearer on our television set than it did in LaFontaine.

That was a big deal for an 11-year-old with three channels to choose from on his Emerson console color TV. Not many had color televisions in the early days, but Dad sold Emersons—so we did!

The *Today Show*, with Dave Garroway and the chimpanzee J. Fred Muggs, instantly became part of our pre-school preparation. The *Today Show*'s ability to show us temperatures from across the USA fascinated me. I thought that 1950s technology was something. I had never heard of Youngstown or Eau Claire until the *Today Show* started informing me what the temperature was in those cities.

What my brother and I enjoyed most were the back-to-back showings of the Three Stooges and Bozo the Clown.

Bozo passed out birthday wishes every day. And Dan and I thought it would be great fun if we sent in a postcard saying we wanted to wish our German Shepherd, Jill, a happy fourth birthday. Naturally, we omitted the fact that Jill Emrick was a dog.

I can picture my brother standing in the doorway, with his baseball uniform on, waiting for Bozo to wish "good little boys and girls" a happy birthday. Dan wasn't leaving until the birthdays were read.

When Bozo announced that "Jill Emrick of Wabash is four today," Dan raised his fist in celebration. It was as if he had just cleared the right-field porch at Yankee Stadium. Only then did he triumphantly stride out of the house and climb into the car to head to the baseball diamond.

We thought running a harmless con on Bozo was hilarious.

In my childhood, NBC seemed as American as baseball and fireworks on the Fourth of July. Founded in 1926 as a radio broadcasting network, NBC is America's oldest major broadcast network. The television network launched in 1936, meaning it is 10 years older than I am.

I am, however, older than the peacock, which debuted as a logo in 1956 when I was becoming increasingly interested in broadcasting.

Can't say that I was thinking about Bozo or the Three Stooges or my childhood enjoyment of NBC when Sam Flood asked me, over lunch near 30 Rock, to work as NBC's primary hockey broadcaster in 2005. But when I look back, it seems fitting that I've spent the last section of my career working for such a historic network.

When NBC received the rights to broadcast hockey in 2004, the NHL was in its darkest hour.

Perhaps that seems melodramatic. But after the NHL canceled the 2004–05 season, that's how it felt for those of us working in the hockey world.

The one bright spot was commissioner Gary Bettman granting permission for then Detroit Red Wings player Brendan Shanahan to hold a convention to discuss an overhaul of the rules.

The convention had people representing different areas of the game, including players, owners, managers, officials, coaches, and broadcasters, among others. The latter group included my broadcast partner John Davidson and my new NBC boss, Sam Flood.

Their recommendations, made on December 7, 2004, included:
- Elimination of ties through a shootout. (Happened.)
- No-touch icing. (Happened, although not right away.)
- Streamlining the size of goaltending equipment. (Happened, in stages.)
- Crackdown on obstruction. (Happened.)

- One-minute penalties in overtime. (Did not happen, although it is used today in the 3-on-3 All-Star format.)
- Two-minute penalties for shooting the puck in the stands from the defensive zone. (Happened.)
- Tag-up offside. (Happened.)
- Moving the net forward to create more space behind the net. (Happened.)
- Creation of designated area for goalies to handle the puck and other areas where they can't handle the puck. (Led to the creation of the trapezoid.)
- Wider blue lines. (Tried in preseason, but didn't stick.)

The group had a good batting average when it came to changing the rules.

Flood had proposed allowing in-game television interviews of coaches and stationing a television reporter between the two benches.

I was skeptical that it would produce the desired results. Coaches are guarded at the best of times. I didn't believe they would give away vital information in the middle of a game, with a live television camera on them. I didn't see us learning much that we could use on air from between the benches.

But I was mistaken. We have gathered plenty of quality information and generated good television moments through these revolutionary changes. What most people don't know is that we had a dress rehearsal for these changes, on January 12, 2006, at Detroit's Joe Louis Arena, before we went live with them.

Pierre McGuire would be "Inside the Glass" for the game between the Philadelphia Flyers and Detroit Red Wings. We broadcast the game as if it was going live on NBC, but the public never saw it. We did this to give us a chance to see how we would mesh together.

NBC had hired John Davidson as my broadcast partner, reprising the roles we had at Fox. But JD couldn't participate in the dry run because he was emcee of Mark Messier's jersey retirement ceremony at Madison Square Garden on the same night.

My former Devils partner Peter McNab had been brought in as Davidson's stand-in for the test run.

Producer Sam, the man who had recommended that NBC executives Ken Schanzer and Dick Ebersol hire Davidson, McGuire, and me, was the innovator who came up with the idea of stationing a broadcaster near the benches. The person stationed inside the glass would be allowed to report what he saw, within the boundaries of good taste. He was also going to interview the coach on the bench during a TV timeout. Prior to that, the network only interviewed players briefly between periods.

McGuire is an effervescent former NHL coach with an encyclopedic command of hockey's people, places, and events. He's a world traveler from numerous scouting trips and broadcasts of junior and world tournaments.

Newly hired Red Wings coach Mike Babcock seemed like the perfect coach to test our new in-game bench interview. As we now know, few coaches can do an interview during the chaos of the game quite like Babcock. Once when his Red Wings were in a rare first-period malfunction at Joe Louis Arena, Babcock was live, telling Pierre, "It's pretty simple what's gone wrong here. We're going up the middle with our passes out of the D-zone, not off the boards." At precisely that moment, future Hall of Fame defenseman Nicklas Lidstrom passed errantly up the middle. And, without a pause, Babcock added, "And right there, our best player, just did the same thing. But we'll adjust and we'll be okay."

To get the hang of how this new broadcast team would blend together, Pierre's microphone was controlled initially in the production truck. I'd hear Sam whisper in my ear that "Pierre can add" and we would bring him into our conversation. The result was largely seamless. That was our rhythm, choreographed by Sam, through that first playoff, when the Carolina Hurricanes defeated the Edmonton Oilers in seven games to win the Stanley Cup.

Even in that first dress rehearsal, we could tell that stationing Pierre near the benches would yield a more intimate understanding of the game's temperament. He could hear when tempers were rising and tensions growing.

We learned some other truths in our dress rehearsal, such as the fact that players closest to him were listening to him, just like he was listening to them.

The day after our practice broadcast, we were standing by the boards and Red Wings forward Kirk Maltby walked by and said: "Awesome stuff last night, Pierre."

If a player believed we had "awesome" material, we assumed the fans would love it as well.

That turned out to be the case.

During one game in Boston, there was a potential goalie interference play resulting in a goal for the Bruins. The play could have been challenged by Alain Vigneault, coach of the Rangers, but was not. Upstairs, Eddie Olczyk, who by then had taken over for JD in the booth, thought goalie Henrik Lundqvist should have sold it a little more if he felt he had been interfered with.

Before the second period started, we noticed Vigneault talking with the referees. The visiting coach is always the in-game interview in the second period and Pierre's question was direct to the point: "Why didn't you challenge?"

Vigneault said he knew that if he was wrong, he would lose a timeout that might be valuable later. He thought the video information he had wasn't clear. That's why he had not challenged the call. And he told us that the conversation he had with the officials between periods convinced him that the officials probably would not have reversed the call. In his mind, he had made the correct decision.

Without the "Inside the Glass" perspective, we wouldn't have received that information.

Eventually, rather than having to always say "Pierre can add," Sam gave Pierre an open mic. But he also had a cough button, mostly to prevent unwanted language.

The NHL and NBC were brought together by mutual love for the sport and, of course, a drive for making money. That is the genesis of outdoor hockey games. Many successes of the Winter Classics and Stadium Series and Heritage Classics came after.

One of my favorite outdoor memories was exploring the scoreboard at Fenway Park as part of the pregame tour. I discovered that the ladder enabling park attendants to take home runs out of the screen—which used to sit atop the Green Monster—was still there. I also learned that the normal yellow numeral used for in-inning scores would not be used for in-period scores the next day.

"We only have one yellow number 1," I was told. "What happens if both teams get a goal and the period isn't over? We'd be stuck."

I guess they would. You must think about everything when you change over from baseball to hockey.

USA Hockey and Hockey Canada both wound up with Hockey Day in their respective countries. Our Hockey Day in America celebrations were outstanding, with terrific stories being told at such sites as outside the Olympic Arena, on the old 1932 and 1980 speed skating track in Lake Placid, New York.

On Hockey Day in America in 2019, in Minnesota, we had Zach Parise of the Wild provide his youth hockey jersey and Pat Maroon of the Blues bring his. Maroon wore No. 7 as a youngster, the same number he was wearing for the Blues.

Perfect!

Some people say All-Star Games lack luster, but I have fond memories from recent games. As previously mentioned, I was able to sit at a table at the All-Star Game in Los Angeles with retired greats Bobby Orr, Wayne Gretzky, Mario Lemieux, and active players Sidney Crosby and Jonathan Toews.

I also have fond memories of Kendall Coyne-Schofield competing favorably against the NHL All-Stars at the 2019 game in San Jose. I also won't forget tough guy John Scott winning the MVP award at the All-Star Game in Nashville. It was touching to see Scott's family near him as Pierre McGuire interviewed him.

Shortly thereafter, NBC allowed me to host a roundtable including five of the eight living members of the 1960 men's gold medal Olympic hockey team. The interview was done in Squaw Valley, California, where the Americans had won their gold.

What struck me from that interview was forward Weldy Olson's recollection that they were given one dollar a day in expense money.

"Yes, they gave it to us all at once," Olson said.

That $17 had to last the entire Olympics.

They were indeed amateur players. Jack Kirrane tucked his gold medal into the glove box of his pickup truck and went back to work as a fireman in Brookline, Massachusetts. John Mayasich returned to work the next day as an advertising salesman for a radio station.

MY TIME AT NBC HAS been immensely fulfilling. We are not only colleagues at NBC, but friends as well. Former NHL goalie Brian Boucher
joined us in 2018 and immediately showed a knack for television.

He speaks at a listenable pace, and he can put you in the mind of
both the goalie and the shooter. His analysis is quick and authoritative.

Even with no previous television experience, he fit well with Olczyk
and me. We had no on-air collisions when it came to talking. You could
tell immediately that he was destined for a lengthy career in television.

Away from the camera, Boucher constantly amuses us with his hilarious impersonations of famous hockey people.

At NBC, the people I work with seem more like close friends or
family than colleagues. When you work as long as I have with these
people, a mutual respect develops.

I have the utmost respect for Sam's vision of how we should present
the NHL to our viewers. I also appreciate that he gives me a license to
let me be who I am as an announcer. That sometimes means paying
homage to the minor leagues. We try to work in a picture of the minor
league champions during the NHL playoffs. We even talked about the
Federal League, where the Carolina Thunderbirds set a record by losing
only six games in regulation. They were 49–6–3.

People don't seem to believe there's a connection between those
leagues and the NHL. But as a former minor league broadcaster, I can
attest that there are plenty of connections. Having ridden those minor
league buses, I like to promote the minor leagues when I can.

The NHL owes the minor leagues thanks because they introduce
many people to the sport for the first time.

That's what happened to me. If not for the presence of the Fort
Wayne Komets, I might not be where I am today.

That's why I will drop in a minor league tale now and then to a
playoff broadcast. During the 2018–19 playoffs, I explained that former

NBA player Popeye Jones was dividing his time between his son Seth's NHL games with the Columbus Blue Jackets and Seth's brother Caleb's AHL playoffs game with the Bakersfield Condors.

Their dad had watched defenseman Caleb's quadruple-overtime loss to the San Diego Gulls in the opening game of the Pacific Championship. It ranked among the top 10 longest games in AHL, taking more than five hours to complete. But the elder Jones arose the next day and flew back to Boston to see Game 5 between Seth's Blue Jackets and the Bruins.

Those are the kind of minor league–NHL connections I like to report on air.

Countless people have helped me along the way and I wish I could thank all of them. I have done my best to do so in cursive writing on paper, using snail mail. I think it helps to slowly enter my thoughts on paper, and people rarely receive first-class mail anymore that isn't a bill. Plus, the Postal Service can use the money.

Lee Anne Marks has kept all of us from getting lost before and after so many games. As our talent coordinator, she knows and is greeted with smiles by people of every rank in all the arenas we visit. Things move smoothly, thanks to this lady from Arnie Palmer's hometown.

Ben Bouma is the NBC statistician/editorial consultant. Fellow NBC broadcaster Kenny Albert calls Bouma the "IRG," or the "Information and Rules Guru."

Throughout every broadcast, Bouma is by my side, slipping me information that I can use on air. Whenever I talk about how long the Detroit Red Wings have gone without a shot or that Braden Holtby has gone 2:34:29 without giving up a goal, it's because Bouma has done the quick addition for me.

He's been the instigator of plenty of fun in the broadcast booth, like the time in January of 2015, when we were broadcasting in Washington, and I was assigned to start the buildup for the Kraft Hockeyville contest, where a local rink is selected to be the location of an NHL preseason game.

After I read the promo spot, Pierre and Eddie started talking about local rinks that might be worthy candidates.

It was well established that our group had enormous affection for the movie *Slap Shot*. And Bouma also wanted to keep the conversation going. That's why he wrote down on a note card: "What about the ol' War Memorial?"

Built in 1950, War Memorial Arena in Johnstown, Pennsylvania, is where *Slap Shot* was filmed.

The suggestion made me smile and prompted me to use my Jim Carr impersonation and bring up Bouma's suggestion on air.

Carr, played by Andrew Duncan, was the broadcaster character in that movie. I'd done the impersonation before, but not in front of a national audience. It was all in good fun. But our impromptu discussion of War Memorial led to a groundswell of support for the arena. Eventually, War Memorial won the contest and we did the first Hockeyville game from Johnstown the following September. The Tampa Bay Lightning and Pittsburgh Penguins were the teams involved. I dressed up like Carr and Lightning coach Jon Cooper dressed up like Reggie Dunlop (the character played by Paul Newman).

Bouma and other members of our crew can impact our broadcasts.

The studio show is anchored by the erudite Notre Dame alum Liam McHugh or the former Rutgers 3,000-meter steeplechase record-holder Kathryn Tappen. Both are top-line performers. The longtime former NHL patrol officer on wing, Keith Jones, is the voice of reason as an analyst. He's the "glue" of the intermission and the unvarnished Mike Milbury is the gadfly. That's the role Mike has played throughout his career as a player, coach, general manager, and broadcaster. I will always admire Mike's courage in standing up as a player rep and questioning the moves of eventually imprisoned NHL Players Association executive director Alan Eagleson.

While Eddie Olczyk was sidelined by his cancer treatments, Mike was my color commentator. It was never dull working with him, hearing his many stories, and getting his frank appraisal. During our telecast on which we showed the last remnants of Joe Louis Arena being dismantled, he candidly observed, "Fine! It was a dump when it was opened, and it's a dump coming down."

Among the subjects we would discuss away from the rink was professional wrestling. Mike remembered the time that towering Andre the Giant (7-foot-4, 520 pounds) came by Boston Garden and was photographed holding up Bobby Orr on one arm and Derek Sanderson on the other. Later, while walking around Columbus, Mike discovered a miniature Andre the Giant statue (about six inches high), an antique toy with a $30 price tag. He presented it to me on camera as a gift.

I was stunned beyond words.

AS WE GROW OLDER, WE all grow more sentimental about careers, our family, and our lives in general. I'm no exception. Emotion has gotten the better of me a few times while I've been live on the air.

Once, the Detroit Red Wings were hosting former team masseur Sergei Mnatsakanov and defenseman Vladimir Konstantinov after they had been severely injured in an automobile accident. They were sitting in owners Mike and Marian Ilitch's suite one afternoon in Joe Louis Arena.

The ovation for the two of them was so strong after a commercial break that I was overcome.

That has happened to me a couple of other times when we carried the national anthem live from Chicago. The presence of service personnel on the ice, particularly elderly ones from World War II, always gets to me.

In every case, it took me just a few seconds to recover.

With seven Emmy Awards, including a record six in a row, it is impossible for me to have anything negative to say about my career. I've always felt blessed.

Sam Flood has taken care of me for plenty of years. It is always enjoyable to work at a place where you have the boss in your corner. No matter what is going on in my life, I know Sam has my best interest at heart.

That has meant so much to me. It also has meant much to me that NBC has allowed me to be a voice beyond play-by-play and to be creative.

After the tragic bombing of the Boston Marathon in 2013 and when Gordie Howe passed away in 2016, Sam asked me to deliver words that reflected the network's sympathies. It means much to me that Sam asked me to do that.

Sports are supposed to provide a distraction from our everyday worries. But in recent years, the sports world has been at the intersection of tragedy. It's disgusting that we are forced to deal with many shocking, tragic events. But I believe we've seen goodness in the face of the horror. In my opinion, goodness has been in the majority.

I remember seeing that goodness after the Boston Marathon bombing. Of all places, I saw it at the Devils-Rangers game at Madison Square Garden.

A pane of glass happened to break in that game, and we immediately went to commercial break. When it wasn't fixed after we came back live, I didn't have anything enlightening to say. Neither did Pierre or Eddie. At that moment, the Garden's event coordinator chose to play Neil Diamond's "Sweet Caroline" over the sound system.

Everyone in the New York crowd understood that the song was associated with Boston sports. Boston teams were rivals. On another day, playing that song would have drawn boos. But not on this day.

Fans started singing along in support of Boston, a town that had experienced a major tragedy.

Our director, Jeff Simon, began showing closeups of the fans singing. As the song neared its completion, the camera settled on a woman who had dared to wear a Bruins jersey to a Rangers game. She was also holding an American flag. Jeff stayed with her as she blew a kiss, and you could read her lips saying, "Thank you, New York."

It was a wonderful moment. The glass was finally fixed and we went back to Devils-Rangers hockey.

But the moment has been captured on YouTube. And I will tell you when I want to remember the goodness that is present in our souls, I go back and watch that video. It inspires me.

Our crew has created an atmosphere in which I get to have fun.

Instead of just signing off, "For Pierre McGuire and Eddie Olczyk, this is Mike Emrick saying, good afternoon from the Wells Fargo Center," I started adding the names of obscure former players from the teams involved.

When the Penguins were playing the Flyers, for example, I would say, "For Pierre McGuire, Eddie Olczyk, Josef Melichar, Jiri Latal, Battleship Kelly, and Sandy McCarthy, this is Mike Emrick saying, good afternoon from the Wells Fargo Center."

I enjoy using the names of tough guys.

I have been given the gift of being able to broadcast NHL games by ESPN, ABC, Fox, and NBC. But, by the evolution of the sport, its changing rules and speed, and my growing into, I hope, a better announcer, my most enjoyable years have been the last 15 with NBC.

THE LAST
ELEVATOR RIDE

When I started dreaming about being a professional hockey broadcaster, my game calls were recorded for an audience of one.

Those were my Fort Wayne Komets play-by-play practice tapes, created in the 1960s with the hope that I could listen later and learn from my mistakes. A couple of those tapes still exist.

I never considered that in 1969 I would send tapes of those calls to minor league teams all over the country. I could not have guessed that then Port Huron Flags owner John Wismer would retain the tape and then four years later offer me my first play-by-play job. I never considered that my job with the Flags would be the launch pad for a career that would span nearly 50 years and include the minor leagues, NHL, NFL, the Olympics, water polo, and everything in between.

My one-game reach grew from one to 27.6 million. That was the average viewership for my NBC broadcast of the 2010 Olympic gold medal game between Team USA and Canada from Vancouver.

The NBC broadcast of Stanley Cup Game 7 between the St. Louis Blues and Boston Bruins in 2019 had a peak audience of 10.4 million.

Where I've ended up has been humbling for a man who started at a 250-watt radio station in a city of 30,000 in Michigan's thumb. Port Huron, Michigan. 1973. The International Hockey League. Larry Smith was my color analyst, but only for home games. When the team traveled, I performed solo.

In 2019, I went to breakfast with Smith and Bill Watt, who played for that Flags team in 1973.

"So how long you going to do this?" Watt said, looking away, not making eye contact.

He sensed the question would make me uneasy.

"I don't know," I said staring into half eaten oatmeal with brown sugar. "I still really like it."

When you are 73, that question is as sensitive as it gets. It's not a subject you enjoy thinking, or talking, about. You don't want to outstay your welcome. But you don't want to leave with any chance of regret about your decision.

"You will know," Smith said with a knowing smile. "You will know when it's time."

"He's right," Watt said.

Both men have been retired for some time.

Two people have been charged with letting me know when I may have avoided the stage hook for one shift too long: Lou Oppenheim and Eddie Olczyk. That is, if I don't figure it out myself.

Eddie is a close friend and a pro's pro as an analyst. He will always be a good judge of the quality of my work. We have shared enough joy and hardship in our lives that I'm confident that he will be able to handle this difficult discussion.

Eddie has stared down cancer. He can tell an elder broadcaster when it's time to ride off into the sunset.

Oppenheim has served as my agent and friend for many years. Art Kaminsky had assigned former actor Dennis Holland to be my agent in the 1980s. Holland had once been in the cast of a Broadway production with Dick Van Dyke and had a photo on his desk to prove it.

Dennis expertly steered Bill Clement and me into the five-year contract with the Flyers and had skillfully handled all the questions about my cancer and when I decided to not work during the 2002 Olympics in Salt Lake City.

But Dennis was still a performer at heart and left shortly thereafter to return to acting.

Enter Oppenheim. Calling him "my agent" falls short of describing how important he is to me.

When I was writing about the Pittsburgh Penguins for free in 1970–71, there was a specific interview with coach Red Kelly that has stayed in my memory for these many years. Usually, a half dozen writers would talk to Kelly after a game. But the Penguins were playing poorly, and after another bad loss, the postgame media contingent consisted of me and famed Pittsburgh Steelers announcer Myron Cope, who worked for Channel 4.

Kelly had won eight Stanley Cup championships as a player. He had seen it all in the NHL.

Seeing there were only two of us, Kelly said: "My father always said, 'When things are bad, you can count on one hand the number of people who are there.'"

Kelly wasn't just talking about how many reporters had showed up for this game. I've always thought about Kelly's quote when I've taken stock of the important people in my life. When I get down to the people I can count on, Oppenheim always makes the cut.

When it comes to health issues, career decisions, forks in the road, and personal dilemmas, Oppenheim has been there for me with sound advice. He represents my interests with finesse and, when necessary, with authority.

It's only been in recent years that I've allowed myself to be relaxed about my career. The late Bob Chase always encouraged me to be myself. But worrying about accuracy is who I am. I just can't accept anything less than perfect when it comes to identifying players or accurately describing what's happening on the ice.

Even though intellectually I understand that mistakes are inevitable, it still eats at me when I goof up a call. I've been known to slam my hand on my notebook when I misidentify a player in front of millions.

It's often been Oppenheim pulling me back from the edge in those situations.

I call the people I can count on my Iron Five. They include Oppenheim, Olczyk, Sam Flood, my wife, and my brother, Dan.

Throughout my life I've met many good people, but Dan is the best person I ever met. Loyal. Polite. Devout. If you need a favor from him, the answer is always yes. He does the bookkeeping for my 95-year-old aunt and runs errands for his neighbors. He was a high school coach, and one of my regrets is that I never got to see him coach. We always saw each other out of season because we had our busy periods from September until June.

My brother said people have always asked him whether he wished he would have become a broadcaster, and he always tells them: "No, but I wouldn't have minded being my brother's agent."

Joyce has always been a guiding light in my life, which is fascinating when you consider that for the first couple of years we were dating we both assumed we would never marry each other.

I was committed to pursuing an NHL career that meant moving outside of Michigan. She loved living in Port Huron and didn't want to leave.

But when we were apart for only a few months after I took the job with the Maine Mariners, I was sure I didn't want to get along without her.

It must have been incredibly difficult to be the one staying home while I was globe-trotting for my job. In the years I was broadcasting 120 games per year, she was alone 150 to 175 days a year. I don't have a true grasp of how lonely that must have been at times. But she found a way to alter her life by diving into friends, dogs, horses, and family when I am gone.

She is such a kindhearted person, and I have numerous stories to prove that fact. When her nephew was a music student at the University of Michigan and became interested in learning about life as a Broadway musician, he began corresponding with a fellow trombonist in the New York production of *Jekyll & Hyde*. Joyce took it upon herself to pay for her nephew and her to fly to New York. They met the musician at the stage door and our nephew sat in the pit orchestra and was invited to play along the entire second act.

If Joyce wasn't such a charitable person, that meeting never happens.

She has been like that since the day I met her. My parents lived on less than five acres in rural Indiana, and the first time I brought her home to meet them, she volunteered to clean out the sheep shed.

My mom kept pet sheep and raised lambs for kids to adopt for 4-H projects. In the winter months, the sheep shed became manure-ridden and smelly. It was an ugly project to clean it out in the summer. But Joyce said we would do it and we did. She earned innumerable bonus points from my parents for that work.

And after that experience, we decided, no sheep for us.

We would sometimes secure a suite when I broadcasted games in Detroit and would invite our friends. While I was on air, Joyce would serve as host for 30 or more guests.

One year I told our guests that our party would be in February, but I said I didn't know whether Joyce would be there because it might be after she heads to Florida. One of our guests said to me: "I like it so much better when Joyce hosts."

Joyce doesn't watch my games anymore—after 47 years in the business—though she will often watch the on-camera segment of the open to see how I look and if the suit, shirt, and tie match. She has a vested interest in that because she picks out all of them. Then, it's likely back to HGTV, the History Channel, *The Incredible Dr. Pol*, or one of the other shows featuring veterinarians.

The ironic aspect of our marriage and career has been that my rise to become a high-profile broadcaster allowed us to have one thing she wanted from that first date in 1974: a life near the nice water in Michigan.

What I can say about my life with Joyce and my career is that time has passed too quickly.

I remember my first game was Port Huron at Toledo with Bill Watt on the ice in October 1973. And, I will know when my final game will be. Unless I have a catastrophic stroke or massive event which comedian George Carlin always described in a New England accent, "You heah about JOOr-gggg? He had a myocaadial infahction!"

I hope my final game will be after the Stanley Cup is handed out in some meaningfully silent losing-side town or thunderously elated winner's city.

In 2012, after an Emmy celebration, Sam Flood told me that it would be up to me when I left. Nobody, or hardly anyone, in network television receives that deal.

But he told me it will be my call. When you reach my age, you often preface your proclamations with "God willing" or "God only knows." To me, it's not a superstition but a growing realization.

I can only guess how I might feel when I take the last elevator ride up to the press box to call my last NHL game from a still-to-be-determined location, and then the last ride after.

While watching Ken Burns' PBS series on country music, I heard one artist, asked to compare the past and present, say: "You cannot put your foot in the same river twice."

The point is that a flowing river constantly changes, and the second time your foot goes in it's a different experience. The point: if you refuse to be happy unless your world remains the same, then you end up a grumpy old man.

I have always accepted the changing NHL river. My enjoyment of the sport has evolved over time. But I also admit that I enjoy that there is continuity between the past and present in the hockey world.

I love that one of the leading Flags scorers in my first season in Port Huron, Ray Germain, had as heavy a sweat-laden jersey at the end of his night as Connor McDavid has today. Conditioning rituals have changed. But this game still requires a centerman to play all 200 feet.

I love that a player on the 1973 Port Huron Flags, probably earning $325 a week for 22½ weeks, reacted the same to an important goal as then Toronto Maple Leafs forward Tyler Bozak did when he scored the shootout winner in front of more than 100,000 fans at Michigan Stadium in 2014.

"The fans were great—seemed to really be into it, didn't they?" Bozak said.

Guys in the minors said the same things when they were playing in front of 3,000 people. Whether a hockey player is earning hundreds or millions of dollars, he always appreciates the fans.

I love that the dressing room ambience is the same today as it was in the 1970s. And it's a dressing room, not a locker room, because players have stalls or cubicles, not lockers.

In a hockey dressing room, players, for the most part, still look you in the eye and answer your questions, just like they did when I was working in the IHL. The only difference is they have more teeth now, although you still don't find many flawless dental charts in the NHL.

I love that the game's roots are in rural Canada. That means young stars use their first signing bonus to buy their parents something nice. Years ago, it was a car. Today, it's a house.

I love that hockey is such an international sport that Flyers forward Jake Voracek, a Czech native, played an NHL game 10 miles from his hometown in 2019. He bought 90 tickets to get all his friends and family into the game. It wasn't cheap.

His parents, Milo and Hanna, watch all their son's games on television. With the time difference, the local start time is 1:30 AM. They end at 4:15 and then the Voraceks go to bed. It had to be a lifetime thrill to have an NHL game to watch "in person" in prime time.

When the NHL finally published the salaries of its players in 1988, there were two players making over $1 million: Wayne Gretzky and Mario Lemieux. Entering the 2019–20 season, 26 players are making $10 million or more and 465 are earning $1 million. The average NHL salary is around $2.8 million.

What remains unchanged is that the sport is still full of givers, not takers. Without being browbeaten by teams to "go do something for charity," NHL players have a tradition of being givers even when the cameras are not on them. They don't have to be celebrated for their charitable acts. In fact, they prefer to be anonymous. No cymbal crashes required.

I love that.

What I don't love is commissioner Gary Bettman being booed in every public appearance. He is a man who has saved at least a dozen franchises from transfer or other plunder. He may not care. But if the fans in these cities knew how he had saved the team they so lustily cheer, they'd tone it down.

I recall thinking when Pittsburgh and Nashville were in the Stanley Cup Final, were it not for Bettman, we could have been seeing Kansas City and Hamilton.

I don't love that the standard for uniform numbering has reached the point where a fan in the upper tier can't identify the players by their sleeve numbers. These fans pay dearly for their seats—probably a higher percentage of their after-tax income than people in the lower bowl. They deserve to be able to know who is on the ice.

Of course, almost all broadcast locations are above the second tier. Hence, I have a selfish interest in this issue.

I know some people in the sport are concerned about this. When Lou Lamoriello was general manager in New Jersey, he asked some office staff one summer to don the prototype new black-red-and-white Devils jerseys—home and road—and go down on the cement floor of the Meadowlands Arena. They were told to "keep moving." While they were walking around, team executives climbed into the top tier to see how well numbers could be read on the back of sleeves. This was a much better test than holding the jersey on a hanger in a vice president's office and hearing, "Looks good!" The normal sleeve number is four inches high. It seems only fair that you should be able to see that number if you pay to get in.

But mostly I love putting my foot in the river in this sport.

In 1980, I was thrilled with anticipation of broadcasting my first pre-season game, between the Canadiens and Flyers at the Spectrum. Larry "Big Bird" Robinson. Guy Lafleur. Bob Gainey. Bill Barber. Bobby Clarke. These were players on television when I was in Portland. Now they were going to be on a television screen with my voice attached.

In 2020, I was thrilled to be in the Cotton Bowl in Dallas, where some of the finest players in the world from a multitude of countries would come out on walkways with flames shooting skyward and planes flying overhead. And, I was excited about that too!

Sixty minutes. A puck that is one inch by three inches. The game is primarily the same as it was when I started. You can accurately say players fought more—and had to fight more—when I started. I get it. I was one of those who thought it was necessary. But I don't get caught up in the debate on eras because it cheapens them.

While I admire the courage of the old-time hockey guys, New York Islanders coach Barry Trotz reminded me that we should admire the modern players for the same courage.

"The courage today is in driving the net, in blocking shots, in big body collisions," Trotz said. This in a league where the average player is 6-foot-1 and 200 pounds.

If you count my two years at Bowling Green calling the second periods of games, I have completed 49 winters of broadcasting the sport.

When you've been a broadcaster as long as I have, you sometimes think you have seen it all. But you really haven't.

Surprises are always around the corner. The 2019–20 NHL season seemed like many others until it wasn't. This is how I closed the San Jose Sharks–Chicago Blackhawks NBCSN broadcast on March 11, 2020:

"Final score in the game: the Blackhawks, 6, the Sharks, 2. Darren Dreger will have a further update on an eventful day after these messages."

What Canadian broadcaster Dreger reported was that the NHL season was going on hiatus because of the COVID-19 virus.

I quickly scooped up my game notes and headed out of the broadcast booth. Thanks to Eddie Olczyk, the United Center elevator was waiting on the seventh floor for the express ride to the event level. Then a quick dash out a rear door to Eddie's car. He volunteered to drive me to the Drake Hotel.

There were quick hellos en route, but the regular handshake ritual was missing. We were in a new age. On a normal day, I shake 50 to 75 hands between the morning skate and the end of the night. Not on this day.

The hours before the game had been surreal. New guidelines were introduced by the broadcast division of the NHL: there would be no pregame interviews, no interviews of coaches or players at the bench. Our inside-the-glass commentator, Brian Boucher, was allowed inside the glass so long as he did not have to gain access via the bench. So, he would need to walk on the ice. If there were to be any player interviews before the game, they would need to be in the hallway with the interviewer at least six feet away from the subject.

We all understood. We were uncomfortable with the new atmosphere. No admission to dressing rooms, no cameras allowed. The game drew an announced crowd of 21,275. Midway through the first period, I asked Eddie, a regular at Hawks games, to assess whether it was a normal-sized crowd. He said "for sure" that it was. So we showed the crowd and I reported that the turnout was normal.

But it wasn't a normal night for the NHL or its fans.

That night, the NBA announced that because a player tested positive for the COVID-19 virus, it was suspending its season. Our intermission panel discussed whether the NHL would follow suit. The next day, it did.

Often in this business, events occur that were never imagined. This was one of them.

SINCE I BEGAN MY BROADCASTING career, I lost the parents who took me to my first hockey game. I met, dated, and left behind the love of my life for six months. It was over. Then it wasn't.

Now we've been married for the last 42 years. I have learned how to call a hockey game, but still not perfectly. In the process, I've discovered the best way to do it is to try to *not* do it perfectly.

I have survived cancer. I have experienced the heartbreak of losing several beloved dogs. Not everyone will understand this, but should I be allowed a curious question in the Great Beyond, it will be, "Why don't these beloved creatures receive as much time on earth as humans do?" Many animal lovers in the hockey world have wondered the same.

Smith and Watt are right. I probably will know when it's time to take the last elevator ride. When it happens, I won't have regrets. But I will have a sadness that I won't recover from quickly.

The sadness will come from missing the people I've been around for these many years, and not just the people mentioned in this book. This sport boasts a large collection of wonderful people who have treated me well for many, many years. My career has truly been a labor of love.

In my first autumn without hockey, when I suffer the aches of hockey withdrawal, Joyce will be there to pick up the pieces, just like she has many times before. When I had cancer. When I was fired. When I lost my parents. When Katie passed away. Whenever my life has been turned upside down, Joyce has been beside me. I am overwhelmingly thankful for her presence in my life and career.

What I also know is I have been blessed by so much over these many years. I have been exposed to many people who have made me laugh. The television sports world is a world of candy and toys. But it is important to life. Hospital nurses tell us that the call button isn't pushed as often when a sporting event is shown in a hospital room.

In a post-hockey world, my hope is I will continue to live my life in a positive manner, the way Ernie Harwell, my parents, and others urged me to.

I saw a quote from a writer named Susan Taylor that sums it up: "We have the power to break the cycle of negativity that is fueling a very dangerous world," Taylor said. "It's not only possible, it's why we are here."

All of this was on my mind while this book was being written. One morning, I was paying my daily homage to Hall of Fame defenseman Tim Horton. By that, I mean I drove to the Tim Hortons franchise in St. Clair, Michigan. I enjoy their splendid coffee in the morning.

This was a dark October morning, around 6:00 AM. The sun hadn't come across the St. Clair river from Canada yet. When I returned home and found three sleeping girls—Joyce and our two pups—I went back to bed. I fell asleep and experienced a rare morning dream.

I was walking down the hallway of an empty, unidentifiable arena. All I saw was a progressive series of team photos, one from each season. The team wasn't evident to me. But I kept walking down the hallway looking at the pictures, each further back in time than the previous one.

Some of the last pictures had only a dozen or so players and one goalie. All youthful players with smiles. Their whole lives ahead of them.

I reached the end of the hallway where the last picture was hanging. There was a hand railing there. And I remember pausing with my hands on the railing, having surveyed all the years of pictures. The hallway was quiet. I stood there for a moment. Then I placed both hands over my eyes and cried. I have no idea why. Then, I woke up.

Maybe someday I will understand if that dream holds any relevance or not.

EPILOGUE

Late spring, 2020.

After that elevator ride in Chicago, the NHL went on pause. The world experienced months of trauma. The interruption of the daily performances of sports was only a sidebar to the suffering and death brought by COVID-19.

As this is written, the NHL is attempting, through various phases, a restart.

Any autobiography or history of hockey is not a bound volume but a three-ring binder. God only knows what will be added when I press the button at the bottom of the notebook and pop the three prongs open. But whatever gets added, I am thrilled for what is there already and I look forward to whatever chapters I am entitled to write in the future.

Finally, I am grateful to all with whom I could share time—many mentioned in these chapters—and several mentioned in the acknowledgments which follow.

ACKNOWLEDGMENTS

At the risk of serious omission, among those not mentioned in this book are my loving 95-year-old stepmother, Mary, an inspiration. My dad hit the lottery twice, once with my birth mom, and, after she passed in 1999, a second time with Mary. Another set of encouragers are Joyce's twin and his wife, Bob and Grace Sult, and nephew Ryan Sult and his family.

Many previously not mentioned had faith not only in me but in hockey on television: Joe Cohen (MSG Network), Rick Gentile (CBS), Mike Pearl (Turner Sports), Ed Goren (CBS/Fox), and Dick Ebersol and Ken Schanzer (NBC).

Some wonderful people in my hockey life have passed, and so I hope the memory of Frank Mathers, Brent Hancock, Kenny Hatt, and Steve Summers, great comrades from Hershey, are still strong with their families. The same for the family members of Bob Chase spread across the country from their birthplace in Fort Wayne.

I thank some 50 analysts with whom I have worked in any number of sports. Hockey, football, basketball, water polo, luge, boxing, et al. I wish I could have devoted paragraphs to all of these wonderful men and women.

Numerous fans and fan clubs have been important in their support and positive energy over the years, including fan clubs of the Flags, Mariners, Flyers, Devils, Rangers, and Hershey Bears. I'd